REFLECTIONS

by

Holly Willoughby

For Dan,
Harry, Belle & Chester

C

CENTURY

Contents

Introduction 6

*'I want to share with you a personal ritual…
I like to light a candle to set an intention to
connect with myself, pause for a moment and
create a space that helps me to achieve my goals.
There is endless possibility in the flicker of a
flame and somehow the warm glow feels like
home, even when you're away. So before we
begin, light a candle and take a deep breath…
Now you're ready to turn the page…'*

Hello!

Firstly, I just want to say thank you for picking up this book. I wonder if the reason you were drawn to it was the same reason I started writing it…

Have you ever found yourself in that moment where you just wonder – what's next? Where you think, well, I could carry on as I am, but somehow there's a yearning for something else? Maybe that moment, for you, is right now. That's where this book started for me.

I think the timing of this moment is unique for us all. For me, when my children got a bit older, I could suddenly think about myself a bit more, and there were so many questions, so many answers I was looking for. The need for growth, knowledge. Some internal pull towards growing roots and settling down that wasn't satisfied just by having a physical home.

I wonder if that yearning is a pull from within, a rare moment of intuition bubbling to the surface. I think change and growth find you, no matter how much we run from them, hide from them, mask them with whatever resourceful method that has worked up until now. But change finds you in the end; you can't hold it back. I think the moment we open our eyes and ears to change, it comes more rapidly, and what at first is frightening becomes a part of you and feels safe and better. It's like being in the sea, out of your depth. Not being able to touch the bottom can be scary but as you swim, you realise you can do it, and if you want to go to shallow water and touch the ground, the foundations are there. Then, once you experience change, you realise you want more. This book represents the culmination of many years of change and work for me.

I wanted to understand what it means to be beautiful, in every sense of the word. I wanted to explore what it means to be a woman in this modern world and how I fit into the story. Just to be clear, whenever I reference men and women in this book, I mean anyone who has come to identify as a man or woman. I write from the point of view of someone who has always identified as a woman, but I hope this book will feel relatable to all genders.

This book is all about being free to live as your truest self. I believe that when you are free to be the person you truly are meant to be, and can go about life without fighting to be heard or feeling suppressed by something or someone, then magic can happen. Socially accepted behaviours can channel us through very narrow corridors in life, and I want to expand them, stretch them to the limit, and see what my likes and dislikes are without the distraction of others' expectations.

I want to share with you my toolbox, whether it's little things that have helped, or things that have changed my life completely. It's important to say that I really hope this book will nudge you to find your own tools. What works for me may not be right for you, but if I've learned anything it's to try everything, and if it feels right, then keep it. If it doesn't, then let it go. The greatest skill in life is to be able to tune in and listen to what it is you need and want. No book can tell you how to do that, but I hope this one will help you to explore yourself, to trust in yourself a bit more and not rely too heavily on external influences as your guide.

It made sense for me to not only explore my inner self but my outer self too. Inner and outer beauty are two sides of the same coin, and I don't believe outer beauty can truly exist unless it is underpinned by what's going on inside. I want to ask questions about what beauty really means, to refocus that lens, change how we view ourselves, so that we are back in control of our own narrative. I've sat in the make-up chair for twenty-five years and learned a lot. Make-up and getting dressed up are about creativity and having fun, and in this book I will share some of the knowledge that I have gained from the brilliant experts I have worked with… You'll discover the secrets behind the reflection.

I'm going to be honest. I needed to write this book and, selfishly, it's been helpful for me, a release. But I hope that some of my words will resonate with you, too.

Enjoy!

WHAT BEAUTY MEANS

I started working as a model when I was fifteen years old and, as I write this, I have just turned forty. That's twenty-five years of sitting in the make-up chair. But I'm not bored of it. I still love getting glammed up, I still enjoy the fun, the play of it all and I have been lucky enough to work with some amazing make-up artists who have taught me so much.

What I have started to think a lot more about as I've got older is what 'beauty' actually means to me. When I was in my early teens, copying the makeovers from *Just Seventeen* with my friends, I probably would have said that beauty means glamour and red lipstick and maybe Marilyn Monroe. Which it does, in a way, but that is only a tiny part of the story.

We all want to feel beautiful. We all want to feel like we shine in our own skin. That's completely natural and nothing to be ashamed of. The problem comes when we let other people dictate to us what beautiful is and we focus on how we appear on the outside, the image we present to the world at large, and we stop listening to our inner voice and what makes us feel good on the inside.

I don't think you can have outer beauty without inner beauty too. If you can reach the point where you can understand and accept your inner self then everything you do and all the choices you make will come from a place of honesty and authenticity. You'll be able to let go of all the judgement that is placed on us as women every day and all the judgement and pressure that we pile on ourselves.

Most of us spend so much time worrying about what other people think of us and comparatively little asking ourselves how we are, what we need today. We are bombarded by images of 'perfect' lives and 'perfect' bodies in magazines, on TV and particularly on social media. We see photos that have been airbrushed, photoshopped and had filters applied and so we end up aspiring to some unreal ideal that has nothing to do with who we are as individuals. While we are scrutinising our wrinkles, wishing our nose was smaller or that we could afford those high heels, we are ignoring our own inner truth and inner beauty. Who we are and what we love is being drowned out by all this noise.

There is so much to be said for the ritual of beauty. Putting on moisturiser, painting your nails, doing your eyeliner – you can't really multitask while you do these things and they create a moment in a busy day where you pause and you focus on yourself for a moment. Lighting a candle, running a bath and applying a facemask are all acts of self-care that can bring us back to ourselves. Planning a look, getting dressed up for a party and embracing your own style can be so rewarding – when we do it because it's fun, rather than because we feel it's something we have to do to get to the minimum of what society expects of us. So let's do all these things, but do them from a place of solid ground, a place of kindness and authenticity.

On the one hand, we are told that we have to look a certain way, to be a certain shape, to conform. But on the other hand, we're fearful of being seen to care too much

let go of all the judgement that is placed on us as women

about how we look in case someone says, 'She's always looking in the mirror', 'She's vain.', 'She really rates herself, doesn't she?' All these messages are a form of control, they are used like weapons against women to take away our confidence away and undermine our sense of who we are. There is nothing wrong with wanting to look your best. There is nothing wrong with not caring what you look like. The point is that we have to make our own rules and know – really know – what is important to us, as individuals.

But how do we do this? Life is so, so busy. There are so many decisions to make every day. There are so many things that can drown our inner voice. Now that my children are older, I have some time and I'm finally trying to rediscover who I am in the fullest sense. Yes, it's taken until just a few years ago for me to understand I needed to do this and

I needed to do this and find the time and courage to do it

find the time and the courage to do it. And it's still an ongoing process. In the past, I chose not to listen to my inner voice and I bought into a faster pace of life because it felt 'safer'. With lots of distraction and movement I could avoid reflecting on uncomfortable things or asking myself difficult questions. At one time, life felt like it was getting faster and faster, and running around and spinning plates left no time to consider what might be holding me back from connecting with what I really wanted or needed. My brain didn't have the space. So, like so many of us, I know what it's like to use busyness and overwhelm as a distraction.

I'm writing this book, in a way, to get that voice heard. To finally speak and say how I'm feeling. I want you to know what it's like back here sometimes and I hope that helping myself by sharing my experiences will help you. It might ignite a spark of recognition, help you feel empowered or switch on your intuition. I want to talk about all the stresses that we put on ourselves, all the distractions we use so as not to face up to what's going on inside and all the outside pressures we have to deal with every day. The things that stop making life beautiful. I know we can't make all of this stuff go away, we can't change the world overnight, but we can alter how we feel about it and how we deal with the things that get between us and a true sense of inner beauty.

You can go to the beauty counter in a department store and try out a new look or treat yourself to a facial – of course you can! It's fine to want to look your best. You just need to make sure it's your best, not someone else's idea of what that is. And that comes down to inner beauty. And what I think inner beauty really comes down to is being able to take a deep breath and sit within your own skin without having any judgement of either yourself or others. We need to let all of that go and allow ourselves to be accepting of what we bring to this world. Because letting go of the judgement and the negativity makes space for love and kindness and a passion for everything around you and what you do. That is true beauty and that is what shines out into the world brighter than anything else.

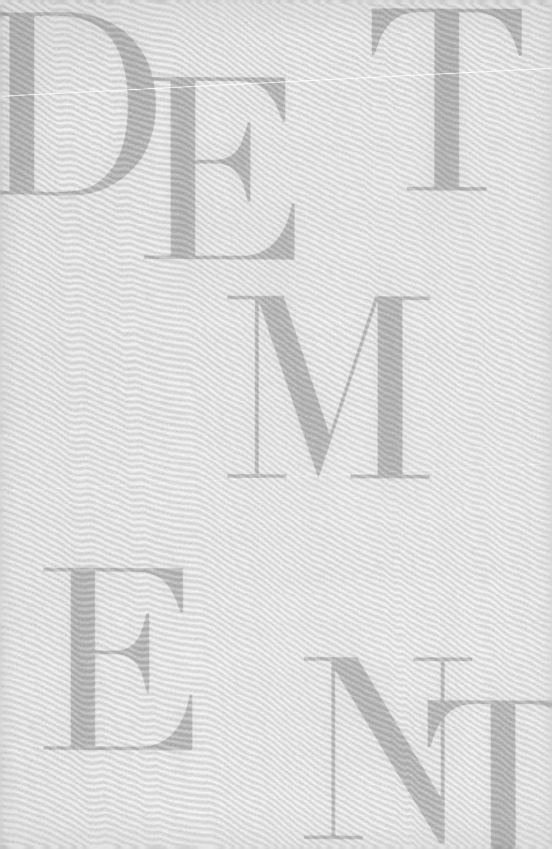

DETACHMENT

Have you ever driven somewhere familiar – to work or your kids' school perhaps – and realised you remember nothing at all of the journey there? You got there in one piece, so your subconscious, used to the habit, must have taken over. Something inside was keeping you safe, and if anything untoward had happened during the journey, you would have come back to full awareness. But switching off like this can still feel dangerous and a bit scary.

Most of us have had an experience like this and will recognise that feeling of 'waking up' and realising you weren't fully present. But this feeling can go beyond the daily tasks we accomplish on autopilot; detachment comes from a deeper place and can seep into all areas of our lives. One day you suddenly discover that, this time, it's not just that you have driven to the supermarket without paying enough conscious attention to the traffic, it's that you're not even present in your own life. This is what I experienced.

I have a lovely life. I'm blessed with a husband I love, three healthy children, wonderful friends and family, and a fulfilling career. Life isn't problem free for anyone; I have down days, arguments and insecurities but I know that I am incredibly lucky. I've always known that. But despite all of this, I wasn't present in my life. Something was missing. There were moments when I felt a bit like a spectator of my own life. I wasn't sad, I wasn't depressed, it was just a feeling of being a little adrift. Although I wasn't unhappy, I felt like I was missing out on *something*.

I've experienced feelings of detachment at moments throughout my life, even as a child. When I was at school, I often found it really hard to keep up in maths. I'm dyslexic and struggle with numbers in the same way I do with words. I was too embarrassed to put my hand up and ask for help, especially as others seemed to find it so easy and it was as if my brain just shut down. I was in the lesson but I wasn't really there. It was a coping mechanism; I was so out of my depth that my brain gave up trying as a way to try to protect me from feeling terrible that I couldn't do it. However, when I was younger, these moments happened only occasionally, in high pressure situations. But, somehow, without my even really noticing it, I was using detachment as a way of coping. From the outside, you'd never have known.

I'm aware, writing this, that as soon as you mention coping, the natural question is to ask 'well, what were you coping with?'. People detach for many reasons at different moments throughout their life; it might be triggered by an upsetting event or it might just build up over a period of time. I'm not going to be detailing what triggered my detachment in this book. I know my triggers; however, I also know my boundaries and talking about it is a hard boundary that I'm not ready to cross. Curiosity is natural, I understand the curiosity, maybe some of that comes from concern and I'm grateful for that. However, over time, I've built my toolkit and finding what works for me has been life-changing. And that's the bit I want to share with you. I think we have a tendency to fixate on other people's stories to distract from our own and that can make us detach even further. I don't want to distract from your story. The journey back to yourself is completely individual.

That doesn't mean that this book isn't deeply personal. It's the most personal project I've ever worked on. I thought about deleting this chapter entirely, not even mentioning detachment, because I knew it would open up a lot of questions. However, it's important to know how to recognise detachment, and to learn how to bring yourself back.

Of course, the realisation that I'd been living this way didn't just fix everything straight away. In fact, I almost felt worse. When I finally understood that I'd been living my life in this autopilot mode, I felt guilty. How could I have wasted all of this time not living my life? I try not to dwell on the past, but time is the most precious thing on this earth. Eventually, though, with some of the techniques I'll talk about in this book, I learned not to blame myself. Now I understand that detachment can even be useful. Our bodies and brains are clever at keeping us safe. Making ourselves numb to bad feelings or upsetting events can be necessary for a short period of time just to help us get through. But detachment can cast a wide net; it can be thrown over our lives without us noticing it, trapping us in familiarity and dullness, not letting us be free to enjoy what should feel really good. It stops us from living life to the fullest.

When you protect yourself too much and keep yourself too safe, you can become out of touch and disengaged.

You end up always looking to the next thing, and the thing after that. Other people might admire how great you look, how stylish your house is, or how much you are killing it at work, but if you feel detached from it all then it's unlikely you will find true contentment. You might have a beautiful life but you aren't present in it.

It's easy to look to the pressures we put ourselves under and the demands that the rest of the world adds to this list to find the reason why we feel detached from our lives. Of course life is fast-paced and often asks a lot of us. But if I'm really honest with myself, I became addicted to being detached yet busy. I suspect lots of other people live this way. We pride ourselves on our multitasking, congratulate ourselves on our ability to be many things to many people – parent, friend, partner, colleague, boss, child – so it's hardly surprising we feel overwhelmed, and I think people become almost used to that. In fact, overwhelm can even be a safe feeling. If lots of other people need your attention, you don't have to focus on yourself and how you really feel. It takes time, energy and bravery to face yourself. I try every day to be more present in my life, and I'll share some of the ways I do that later in this book.

Sometimes it feels like my safest place to be is on the TV. It might sound strange to say that live TV, with all its pressures, is where I feel comfortable, but when I'm working, I can't think about anything other than the job in hand. When we film *This Morning*, I am totally focused. Live television takes no prisoners so you have to be fully present at all times. Sometimes when we say goodbye at the end of the show, it's like bumping back down to earth as I realise I still have to deal with everything I have going on in my life away from the studio. Most people aren't on TV every day, but perhaps you have your own escape. Do you have something you value because it completely takes you away from thoughts, feelings and problems that, if you were honest with yourself, need your attention?

I love my job and will always give it 100 per cent. But I have become more aware of how we can distract ourselves from facing up to things that are making us unhappy. Sometimes it's good to have your mind taken off a problem for a few hours. It might even help you to solve it! But take your mind off it for too long and you end up hiding the cracks forming within yourself. They might be hairline cracks to start with, but in my experience they will always open wide.

It's so easy to put off though, isn't it? When you know that there is something bothering you that you haven't addressed, it's usually for a reason. So how do you get to a place where you are ready to do that? How do you repackage and refile whatever is causing you hurt so it is more manageable, and so you can process it in a way that you learn and grow from?

My light-bulb moment came when I realised that while I couldn't avoid my problems forever, I didn't have to tackle them all at once either. Instead, I think the first

Sometimes it feels like my safest place to be is on the TV

thing to do is to pull yourself back in, bring yourself back into your own body, become more present. You need to examine and face up to how you really feel. You do just have to be a bit brave and put your big girl pants on as, of course, it's not easy. That's why you've been avoiding it! But actually, the more you bring yourself into the present, and into yourself, the braver you become. It will give you a sharp, pinpoint focus, which allows you to make wholly conscious choices. The numbness will start to subside and you can start taking back control and begin to feel what it's like to truly live and be present again. And that's what life is all about.

Of course, addressing what's really going on is going to be more difficult for some than others. It all depends on how deep those cracks run. It takes a certain amount of bravery whoever you are, but I know that sometimes you have to face up to things that you might have been avoiding, whether that's your own bad habits or upsetting events in your life that you haven't truly got over, like a break-up or a bereavement. The process of shining a light into those spaces can initially make everything feel worse, and you'll need to be in a place where you are safe enough and supported enough to do this; seeing a professional is the best way. It may not be a quick process, but when you're ready to do it, that is the right time for you.

Calling this process of coming back to your self enlightenment seems daft and maybe too intense. For me, it felt like healing. It's like coming to an understanding of yourself and who you are in a way that includes the more difficult experiences that you've had, rather than trying to deny them or hide them under a glossy surface. I think it's fair to say that most people have regrets, or moments in their life that they would rather hadn't happened, paths they could've taken but didn't. Our experiences shape us and we can't pretend that they don't.

There is so much out there to enjoy

To be clear, shaping is very different to defining a person. We all have these cracks under the surface that aren't pretty and that we don't like to look at, caused by grief, trauma, fear, shame and disappointment. It's what you choose to do with them that makes the difference. How you use them, how you turn them around, what you learn from them. As scary as it is to look into those dark places, if you can face and unpick the things you find there, this is where you really learn, where you grow from. If you don't ever go there you'll stay consistently in that grey area, you'll remain numb, and you won't get the full experience of life. And there is so much out there to enjoy.

I'm not just talking about serious mental health issues or trauma recovery. We all have different problems covering a huge spectrum. And rather than dealing with them, some people actively choose to numb themselves to a great or lesser – or more destructive – extent, whether by drinking excessively, binge eating or barely eating at all, taking drugs, gambling or having affairs. These are all ways in which we detach and distract ourselves and we become masters at it. Because even despite the pain it may bring to those around us, sometimes in the moment it still feels like the better option, which is extraordinary when you really think about it. How can any of those things be a better option than just sitting still with your thoughts, listening to what's going on, and hearing and dealing with it? Whether you simply think 'life would be better if I didn't feel like this' or you are grappling with a deep-rooted issue that has been with you for years, you deserve to feel better. You don't need to accept numbness and detachment as a way of life. Whatever you're dealing with, you can make changes that will help you reconnect and live more fully.

A turning point for me was when I went to Australia to film *I'm A Celebrity, Get Me Out of Here!* We had a big show to film, which I was hugely focused on, but at the same time, when I walked into the apartment I would be staying in for two weeks and shut the door, I realised I was completely on my own for the first time in years. I didn't have to worry about anyone's bedtime or bathtime, I only had to feed myself. I was in this beautiful country by the beach and I thought, right, I am the luckiest woman alive right now and I am going to make the most of it.

I stayed not far from Queensland's Byron Bay, which is the land of alternative therapies, and I decided that I was going to try whatever I came across. So I went to see a kinesiologist. Kinesiology uses gentle muscle tests to get an understanding of what's going on in your body, not just in terms of the strength of your muscles but also the flow of energy around your body, sometimes called chi. This practitioner was particularly spiritual. She talked to me, asking me questions and performing different muscle tests as she spoke. She intuited things about me that she would have no way of otherwise knowing – about my health, my past, my emotions. Something opened up for me that day. I felt a deep sense of relief within my body that brought me to tears.

When I got home, I used a combination of alternative therapies, dedicated time to working on myself alone and with professional help from a psychologist. I took a deep dive and didn't get better for a while. I would feel like I was finally coming up to the surface and taking big gulps of air, and then I'd go back down and dig around and replay a bit more until I felt confident that anything that was there wasn't overwhelming me or controlling me anymore. I had to shine a light into lots of dark corners, and it wasn't fun but it was powerful, and as I sit here now, I can say it's the best thing I ever did. The psychologist gave me a space to speak openly, feel safe and be heard. Getting an appointment with a counsellor can be difficult but the benefits were invaluable. Seek that friend or family member, call that helpline, join that online group.

For me, alternative therapy played an important part alongside more traditional counselling. However, I am very aware that some people are uneasy with the idea of issues being explored outside of a qualified therapist's office because they feel it's not the safest environment in which to start unlocking things. I can only explain what happened to me.

When I felt safe enough to take the pressure off and let the numbness dissipate, suddenly I was able to feel again – and feel without fear. I took tentative steps to a new normal where I was not numbed, and before I knew it, everything looked a little bit brighter and a little bit lighter. Life's still not perfect, but I have given myself a really good toolkit and I now know what I am capable of.

I don't think you ever completely recover from life's difficult experiences, but you can harness the strong emotions and let them pull you forward. In so doing, you recalibrate, you look within and ask yourself what inner strength, contentment and beauty really mean to you. And I'm guessing it won't be that glossy, outwardly successful façade that you present to the world while frantically trying to keep all the plates spinning and denying how you really feel.

I can cope now with all these things that I've learned from my difficult or detached times, but it remains a work in progress. It's not a straight line, or even a consistently upwards curve towards feeling better. Sometimes you feel worse for a little bit before all the pieces come together and you are able to come back to who you really are and who you want to be. I've had times where I've felt like I've gone downhill. But by facing into my difficulties, I'm definitely feeling the benefit. I know that I am strong enough to do the work needed. I don't think I'll ever get to the point where I'm like, oh yeah, I'm all good now, but funnily enough, I'm not sure I would want to. I'm really enjoying learning and seeing what else is out there, discovering other ways that I can connect to myself, and taking those moments to pause.

And once you start, the world, in all its abundant joy, opens up and you are fully connected.

THE
RACING
MIND

One of the first problems I had to tackle when I decided to reconnect with myself was a racing mind. Even when I tried to pare my schedule and to-do list back so that I could look after myself, it was like my brain didn't get the memo.

A lot of us struggle to sleep these days. I'm a pretty good sleeper but I do have nights where I just can't seem to nod off. My mind races and chases and I think about everything I have to do, everything I should have done... You can do all the right things – not look at your phone before bed, avoid caffeine, have a good night-time routine – but then you get into bed, turn out the light and suddenly you're there with yourself, without any of the distractions you have constantly to hand during the day. Then everything comes flooding in and before you know it, your head is alive with all these thoughts and feelings that you've been running away from all day.

We all know how important sleep is. Endless articles tell us how a good night's rest is vital for energy, to protect our brain, and essential for us to function at our best. But none of that helps when we just can't seem to do it. In fact, the pressure just makes it worse. There are lots of apps and podcasts out there that I know some people find really effective. But I think looking deeper and asking what's really going on when our brain is on such high alert that it won't let us rest might be a longer term cure.

When we've got an endless to-do list and we're rushing around at 100 miles an hour, chasing our tails, we focus on getting through the tasks right in front of us without stopping for a moment to listen to what's going on around us or inside us. What other people are saying or doing, what other people need is the noise that drowns out everything else.

For years I thought: 'I am the best multitasker. I can get all these things done. Look at me go! I can get the kids ready for school with a piece of toast in hand whilst writing that morning's show. I'm having my make-up done while I organise the builder. Look what I can achieve!' It was as though I thought I was going to get some sort of reward at the end of it. But of course, you don't. What happens is that people become used to you being able to function at that level, so therefore more is put on you. Your head gets busier. You get even more tired. Ultimately, you end up doing everything, but doing it all just a little bit badly. You're always living slightly outside your body, thinking about the next thing you've got to deal with, buying concealer to paint over the dark circles under your eyes. Women are famously good at multitasking – we are told it's our superpower – but you know what? Don't multitask. Focus on one job at a time and avoid leaving any one task unfinished. You'll be more content with the results if you do tasks individually, and you might find that you end up getting more done. So slow down and stop living in that state of adrenaline. Put it all back to a level that's manageable, that you can be in control of. And if some things are missed, so be it.

We all have moments when things are a bit much, or too complicated, or the demands on us feel too intense to deal with. We say, with varying degrees of seriousness, 'Oh, I just want to get away from it all.' Or, 'I'd love to escape. I wish I could just jump on a plane!' But imagine if you could simply sit down, shut your eyes and get that same feeling of escape because your mind is no longer racing. If you can pull back and reclaim some of that stillness, you can start listening, and then you can start hearing. And when you hear, that's when the work really begins, and you can really get stuff done, feel the changes and reap the benefits.

Sometimes, it feels as though I have forgotten what it's like for my body to move in a fluid way, without the tension in my shoulders and back, and behind my eyes. Recently, I caught myself feeling so tense that my body felt like a rigid mass just holding me up. So I took a meditation course. It was not something I thought I would ever be able to do, but it's had a huge effect on me. I'll talk more about meditation on page 76, but I'd describe it as feeling like I am taking the power back, creating some space in my head.

The racing mind, the trouble sleeping, the tension in our bodies and the occasional desire to escape is all connected to the state of hyperarousal in which so many of us live.

It makes it hard to switch off, which is why I think a lot of people find it difficult to meditate. Yet that is actually one of the most important reasons to try to find that space in your head. I wanted to lose that feeling, to see if I could just move and flow through life, with everything in balance. More harmony, more peace.

Even if meditation isn't your thing (don't rule it out!), it's still important to find ways to centre yourself and calm your brain. When I feel my head racing, I can sometimes stop it by asking myself a question or giving myself an instruction. This might sound completely off the wall, but if I'm in bed and I can't sleep, I say to myself, 'I'm just going to come out of my head for a bit now, and I'm going to come into my heart. I'm bringing my awareness down into my heart because my head is running around and that's not helping me. I'm bringing myself down into my heart and I'm just going to breathe into that space; I'm going to lie here and just feel that for a bit.' Even as I'm writing this, I can feel the difference that this shift of awareness makes in my body.

Most of us don't like to sit with our thoughts and be 'in' our mind. Apart from the fact that our racing mind won't let us, another reason is that some just equate sitting still with boredom. And maybe they have a point. But actually, by trying to avoid becoming bored, we're missing out on so much. The technology that surrounds us provides constant opportunities for distraction, and numerous different ways to hide from ourselves. Having grown up with this technology, many children never get to the point of being bored because they're bombarded with distractions and influences from all directions. They can always pick up a phone or tablet. I see it with my own children – they very rarely just sit and do nothing. Yet while we worry about our kids having too much screen time and not developing their imaginations, we're no better; I find myself just scrolling through my phone and I don't even know why. It's habitual and addictive, and it means we've lost the art of being bored.

If I think back to when I was a kid and I didn't have anything to do, that was when moments of real fun and creativity would emerge. I would have to think of a game, so I'd say, 'Right, I'm going to make a shop!' and I would live in my imagination for a while. As adults, we need to remember what it was like to be bored, and spend time just sitting, to see what pops into our head. You might surprise yourself. Giving ourselves both space *and* permission to be creative is so important if we are to access who we really are and find contentment within that. And that's a big part of what inner beauty means to me.

One of the reasons it took me a while to come around to the idea of meditation is that I saw it as just sitting still and 'doing nothing', and I didn't think I would be able to. I felt uncomfortable or guilty if I wasn't doing something, wasn't accomplishing a task, working or spending time with my children. Exploring this in more detail, I realised that I definitely like to feel in control and that I have a purpose, and one way I achieve this is by having a huge to-do list of things I can tick off. But what I am really saying to myself is that if I'm not achieving something, if I've not got a job to do or a role to fill, then I'm pointless. That's the message I was unquestioningly giving myself, but that's just not true, is it? You've got to learn to adjust the way you think about things. You have self-worth without having a job to do, and there's a difference between shirking or being lazy and taking the time you need to process your thoughts.

Your body and your skin will thank you if you get a good night's sleep; your muscles and posture will benefit if you can let go of the tension you're holding. But most of all, if you can find a way to sit quietly with your thoughts and feelings, your mind will stop racing and you will be able to reconnect with what's really important.

ANGER

Anger is a powerful emotion. We all feel it at some point in our lives, though for women, it's something we are not really supposed to express. It's an ugly emotion and therefore something we feel we have to deny. When women are angry, they're often seen as 'shrill' or 'hysterical'. Beautiful people are serene and happy is the message, they don't have cause to feel rage. I disagree. Anger might not be something we associate with inner beauty, but I think that refusing to acknowledge anger when we feel it is unhelpful, and takes us further away from our true selves.

Anger is also a complicated emotion that doesn't generally exist by itself – it's closely tied up with other emotions. It often comes from a place of fear, when we feel threatened. Or if we show anger and later feel it wasn't justified, it can lead to feelings of shame – that other people now think less of us because we behaved unreasonably. In this case, we may also feel guilty for being angry with someone who didn't deserve it.

If I try to repress or hold back my anger, it comes out in other ways. Have you ever tried to overlook something or convinced yourself it wasn't important enough to mention at the time, maybe because you didn't want to create a problem for someone, only to find that the anger builds because, actually, it is important? I'd think, 'Well, I won't say anything about that. It's fine. I'll just carry on. It doesn't matter.' There's often a series of moments when maybe you could and should say something, even if it is just expressing yourself, not necessarily disagreeing with someone. But all those little unexpressed bits build up inside and, before you know it, it becomes this great big thing that explodes out of you. Sometimes the trigger for the anger is another small thing and you might even feel bad, like you're overreacting and being unreasonable. But it isn't that individual thing that's the problem but the backlog of tiny moments that have gathered power and energy because you haven't connected with yourself and spoken up about how you really feel. Suddenly it's uncontrollable and overwhelming and you don't know why, but you end up feeling guilty or ashamed.

We all have different relationships with anger. For some people, the anger seems to rise up and flash hotly and quickly. Their fuse is short but they may find it easier to calm down. Some people take a longer time to get angry, but when they do they blow, it's a release. Others find it difficult to admit something has made them angry and they try to ignore it and push it down – perhaps because they're not sure if they have the right to be angry or because they don't want to be seen to lose their temper. Or it can come out as passive aggression – little comments here and there – which can be damaging for relationships. But like all our emotions, if we can understand where anger comes from, it can become a source of growth. Anger's only a problem when it gets out of control, is disproportionate to a situation, or it becomes your overriding emotion, negatively impacting you and those around you.

We do need to be careful how we behave and speak to others when we are angry. It's an unpredictable emotion that can take us by surprise, and we're not always totally in control of what we say in the moment. Wanting to avoid the feeling of being out of control is at the heart of why we shy away from anger. Sometimes we are afraid that we'll say terrible things we can't take back. Of course, despite our best efforts, we might sometimes say something unkind that we don't mean. But apologies can go a long way, especially if you explain where your reaction came from – a place of fear or the transgression of a boundary, for example. It's not true that we can't undo a cross word once said. True apologies that genuinely acknowledge the hurt caused and provide an explanation for your actions can repair rifts. But they require self-reflection.

When I think back on the times I've been angry, often the feeling came from fear. Anger is a close relative of fear. The next time you feel angry, consider whether it's because something about what's just happened scared you. I found myself getting angry at my parents for going to the supermarket during the pandemic because I was scared that they would contract the virus. I got angry at my son the other day when he walked across the road without looking properly because I was scared that he would get hurt. Many of us get angry with our kids when they unthinkingly do something dangerous. Kept in proportion, I think that that sort of anger can be well placed because it's a natural reaction to something and an indication of just how dangerous their actions were!

It's important to try to understand yourself and your reaction, and remember that the things you say or do in anger may be due to fear, rather than your best self speaking. These actions aren't a true reflection of your inner emotions when you're on a much more even keel, and this knowledge may make it easier to forgive yourself.

Once we understand our own anger, we can understand and perhaps become more forgiving of others' outbursts. I've learned when to say, 'I'm just going to walk away. Take a few deep breaths and just think about what you're saying. I understand the point you're making, but let's go back to this conversation in ten minutes, or an hour, or later, or tomorrow, or next week.' Crucially, though, you do have return to it, whether it's you who is angry or someone else.

It is vital to air and discuss the root of any anger, where it has come from. If it does come from fear – whether that's fear of being hurt, of embarrassment, of doing the wrong thing – maybe it's something that you can share and somebody can help you to alleviate your worries or concerns around it. As with all fears, the moment you talk about them openly, the control and power they have over you somehow dissipates. Or if it doesn't dissipate entirely, it subsides and becomes more controllable. I definitely think there is an irony in the fact that we hide away a negative emotion because it feels ugly and unpleasant, yet by leaving it to fester inside of us it actually causes more damage than if we consciously allowed ourselves to air it.

I have to caveat all of this by saying that for some people, anger can be uncontrollable, and can be rooted in something that needs to be unpicked in a safe environment with professional help. But for those of us for whom anger is an emotion that rises up occasionally and may feel scary in the moment but is not overwhelming, I think it is a source of energy that can be harnessed. Feeling anger can be a positive, bringing to the fore an issue you weren't previously aware was so important to you. If you can identify what's making you angry then you can begin the healing process of doing something about it. A burst of anger might trigger a conversation with someone that you've been putting off, hiding from, pushing down, or trying to ignore for a long time. Obviously it's better to own and address these things as they arise, but we all know it doesn't always work like that. Anger might be the catalyst for a discussion that needs to be had or a connection that needs to be made.

What makes me angry has definitely changed over the years. Since I started to consciously tap in to how I really feel, I found myself getting more angry, which surprised me. I wasn't sure if I was comfortable that this anger was part of who I was inside. I now see that when emotions are dampened to protect ourselves, once we start to air them and listen to them, they become so much shinier and brighter. Both the good and the bad. I hadn't reached those heady levels of anger for years because I'd subconsciously chosen to sit in a safe, numbed area.

Injustice became a huge catalyst for my anger, and I still find that I sometimes just have to sit and breathe my way through it. It can be triggered by unfairness that affects me personally, like somebody jumping in on what I said without properly listening to me, or underestimating me in some way. Or it can be a greater injustice out in the world that I see or read in the news, or stories I hear from people I interview. When I was younger, I think my overriding impulsive response to injustice was to cry; now I am more likely to experience irritability. This has helped me to realise the things that I really care about and what makes my blood boil, and it's so good to know these things. What makes you angry? And why?

So what string does injustice pull for me to make me so angry? Where in my life have I felt injustice to such an extent that this is now a real trigger point? Being able to feel my own anger and the situations in which it arose raised lots of questions and, naturally, when you begin to answer those questions, you begin to understand. And when you understand, you learn.

Anger can provide clarity. In my anger, I forget about all of the restrictions that have been placed on me by life – my fear of upsetting someone or hurting someone, or behaving in a way that isn't acceptable to others – and my true voice just comes out singing loud and clear. I can only see this as a good thing. As long as it's not an attack or threat towards someone and it's always done in a way that speaks your absolute truth, then it's a release.

There have been occasions when I have used anger as energy and experienced just how creative and powerful it can be. I was working on a project that was really important to me and indeed everyone involved. I had been working on it and planning it for months. It was an incredibly emotional event and I wanted to do everything in my power to do it justice. I care very much about everything I do and I'd like to think I'm very professional, particularly when it comes to situations that have to be handled in a thoughtful way. Yes, events unfold on screen and there can be some improvisation and lightness, but you always have to get the foundations right.

Then, an hour before I was due on stage, a colleague came into my dressing room to ask how I was and whether I needed any help. I thought that was a really nice thing to do so I explained what I was planning to do and how it was going to work. They went on to tell me that actually, they didn't agree; they thought it would be much better if it was done another way. Their way, funnily enough.

I remember thinking, 'Wow, this is incredible, because I've clearly been thinking about this for a long time and have made a decision based on how I think it should go – and based on all my experience and capabilities as a presenter. And yet this person has just come in and undermined my confidence, based on what they think is a better way of doing things.' I felt sad that this person underestimated me so much, despite all of my experience.

I was also hurt that they hadn't considered that intervening just before I was about to begin work might throw me off kilter, make me feel worried, nervous or insecure, and actually damage what I was doing. Or make me feel incredibly vulnerable, that what I was doing wasn't the right thing, even though I knew deep down it was. And yes, my first reaction was to allow doubt to creep in, followed by some big, powerful emotions tied into the nerves I felt.

This person went on to say that if at any point I was to 'mess up' or not be able to do it, that they would have someone on standby ready to jump in. That really lit the fire and what rose up inside me was one of the most powerful moments of anger I've ever felt. It hurt and it stung. They were gone before I could explode at them, but when they left the room, I cried. I shouted. I called that person every name under the sun that you could possibly imagine, and I could feel my anger pulsating through my body. Now, of course, this was how I viewed the situation in that moment. This person probably had the best intentions. It's only looking back that I can see why I was so angry in that moment: I was carrying a history of feeling undermined and undervalued.

I knew I had to gather myself because I was about to walk out in front of an audience. I couldn't drag that person back into my dressing room to confront them and make sure I was heard when we were so close to going on. So there was no doubt in my mind that I had to harness that energy in a different way.

GUILT

I feel guilty about everything. It's one of the emotions I find hardest to manage. Guilt has been a controlling force over me as a person since I was a child. To this day, I am terrified of being in trouble. I worry about what people think, and for a long time I adapted the way I behaved to limit the guilt that I felt. But by so doing, I have paid the price of not necessarily being my truest, most authentic self.

Shame is often used as another word for guilt, but actually they are different, although connected – like anger and fear. Shame relates to how we feel about the flaws we perceive in ourselves, which can make us think we are bad or broken in some way and isn't usually linked to a specific event, whereas guilt is more about feeling bad because we have hurt someone or done the wrong thing. Shame is a complicated emotion that can go right to our core, so it's an area that requires deeper, more painful exploration and often professional help. The causes of shame need to be dealt with and processed so that you can live with it and it doesn't control how you live your life or the decisions you make. I think shame's best friend is silence; you don't want to speak up, so you keep it all inside and it grows heavier and heavier. The very nature of being ashamed means that you don't want to admit to something, but so often the best thing to do with those things is to look them right in the face and say, 'Right, I'm dealing with you. I'm owning you and I'm not going to be ashamed of this anymore.'

Guilt isn't an emotion that you can stamp out of your life completely

Whereas shame is something that lives deep within us and, at its extreme, makes us feel like we can't ever be beautiful on the inside, I think guilt is so often a form of control, and one that has long been placed upon women by society. I had guilt for being a stay-at-home mum, then guilt for going back to work and not being a stay-at-home mum, and guilt for loving my work. If I love my work, does that mean that I can't love my home life? Must we choose between the two?

I go to work because I love my job. It gives me a sense of purpose. I enjoy doing it and, to a degree, it makes me who I am. It's something I know I can do really well and I think people get enjoyment out of the shows that I do. I earn good money, which means that I can give my family security and buy nice things for my home. And yet I still hear that voice of the working mum's guilt. The voice that says that by going to work you're not spending enough time with your children; that your children are going to have hang-ups and not grow up to be fully rounded individuals because they missed out on some sort of day-to-day contact with you. They will feel they were loved less.

I know that's not true. So why do I still feel that guilt pass over me like a cold shadow? Let's go through it bit by bit: I know exactly why I go to work, and it's certainly not to avoid my children or to 'opt out' of any part of motherhood. Does being a working mum mean I love my children less? Absolutely not. Are my children happy and content and proud of me? Yes, I know that they are. So why do I still feel the guilt?

Here's our old enemy: fear. Fear of judgement is often tied up in a messy package with feelings of guilt. And judgement is another form of control. I feel working mum's guilt mainly because of what's coming in from outside. How I think other people might feel about my working life. But the fact is, I can't change that. If I gave up my job, there would be other people who would judge me for that. So what am I going do? Am I going to hold on to that guilt or am I going to let it go? When you begin to view it in this way, there really is only one answer.

I'm not saying it's easy to turn off those feelings. Like I said, guilt has been such a huge emotion for me over the course of my life, so I understand how complicated and insidious it can be. But I can still look at what I feel guilty about and try to work out where the guilt is coming from. Is it my own or does it come from a set of beliefs that weren't mine in the first place? When I examine the issue, I can see that it's not my guilt to hold. How someone else might feel about me going to work and not being able to do the school run is nothing to do with me. So I'm not carrying guilt that comes from someone else's opinion anymore.

Guilt is an emotion that you can't stamp out of your life completely; you have to learn to manage it, to the point where it's not an overriding feeling. Ask yourself: where are all the places in my life that I feel guilty? What am I feeling guilty for? Whose guilt am I holding? Whose opinion am I holding?

CONTROL

When we reflect on our life journey, we often ask ourselves, 'What would you tell your younger self if you could go back ten years?' Ten years ago, I would have been thirty. I would have had my son Harry and was pregnant with my daughter, Belle. So, firstly, I think I would say to ten-years-ago Holly, 'Don't worry, I know you're exhausted, but it does get better. It's going to take a long time but it won't always be so hard!'

But I also think that the me from ten, or even twenty, years ago has lessons to teach the current me. On one level, I feel better now because I have established what my life boundaries are, but at the same time, I used to be a little less controlling of myself than I am now, and probably more in touch with my intuition.

I don't know whether it's because our baggage isn't yet filled with experiences that weigh us down, or perhaps it's just a strength that comes from innocence and naivety, but it feels to me like I was more in touch with my own intuition when I was younger. I wonder if it's because my own judgement hadn't been clouded by other people's opinions, and so it was easier to know when things didn't sit quite right with me. I definitely think I've clouded my sense of self by letting in too many opinions over the years.

I feel like I am micro-controlled in many areas of my life by others' expectations – of how I should live my life, of things I should and shouldn't do. Judgement is a way of controlling people, and the fear of being judged sometimes stops me from doing or saying something. This is magnified for me because my job takes place in the public eye, but I think it's similar for everyone. We all change our behaviour and make different choices on occasion, simply because we are afraid of being judged. We let other people's opinions – real or perceived – control us.

One of the problems with micro controls is that they are insidious; they are often opinions we have internalised without realising, and so it's hard to point at them, to call them out. This means that our anxiety and sensitivity about them is triggered in other ways, by something that seems quite small and insignificant. For example, if I'm watching something on TV and my husband suddenly asks, 'Why are you watching this shit?', it'll spark something deep inside and I will get disproportionately angry about it. I think it's because all these other screws of control and of judgement have been tightened in ways that I am not always conscious of, and actually a really small, unimportant thing like this sets me off.

So, let's apply our lesson about anger here. If you find yourself getting disproportionately upset or angry about something that seems minor, think less about what actually happened and more about what the situation represents. So in my example, I get angry with my husband when he makes a flippant comment about the TV, but actually I'm angry because I subconsciously feel as though someone's trying to control what I'm doing.

My husband absolutely isn't trying to control me, but I'm getting a really strong reaction, so maybe I'm worried about control in my life. Maybe that's a sign that I still need to address the issue of control.

You can also be too controlled within yourself. Controlling my voice is something I think about often. Sometimes I've played it so safe in order not to be criticised. To fit in with other people's expectations of me, I have ended up simplifying myself and swallowing my voice so that I stay in the pigeonhole I'm expected to sit in. This can mean watering myself down. For example, we might be discussing something in the dressing room before a show, and occasionally I'll voice an opinion to my colleagues that I believe in but decide that I don't want to say on air. The moment you have an opinion or come down hard on one side of a debate or the other, in somebody's eyes it will be seen as controversial or wrong. At the extreme end of the scale, it will offend someone. Remaining neutral is of course a much safer place to be.

The problem is that if I say something in the morning that is deemed to be controversial, then it will be picked up, go online, social media will kick off and then before you know it, it's become a much bigger story – sometimes taken out of context, sometimes not. So I err on the side of caution because I want to go home and be a mum and focus on other things in my life. I want a quiet afternoon, and there is not enough time in the day for me to have to justify myself and my actions.

So I often ignore my own truth. Sometimes that's a pragmatic approach to the job I do, because I need to keep something back for myself. But I have to be careful that I am not giving up my freedom of thought and speech, or watering down how I feel because I'm terrified of what somebody else is going to think. And when you water things down, you start to ignore your inner voice.

Sometimes the chatter in my head is so loud that I'm not even aware of my own inner voice. I find myself almost regurgitating what other people have said because I don't know what I want to say anymore. It feels safer to echo the views of others because it's a tried-and-tested method. To go out on a limb and to speak your own truth can be scary, so it's easier just to use other people's words and thoughts and opinions. But every time you do that, you lose sight of your own. You don't know what you want anymore. You don't know how you feel. I want to be able to hear my own inner voice.

This is part of the reason why, last year, I decided that I was going to manage my own career rather than having a big agency look after my work interests. It was a big decision, but it means that now I'm more in control of what I'm doing on a day-to-day basis. I am more knowledgeable about everything happening in my work, including things that, in the past, other people may have deemed unimportant for me to know. I go to more meetings and have much more first-hand information, and therefore I can make immediate decisions, which makes me feel more present and in control. I made this decision simply for my career, but actually I've found it's helped to pull me back into my own body. I hadn't realised I'd lost a part of me when I gave up responsibility to someone else, but now I am regaining that.

When to let go and delegate and when to take control remains a difficult one to judge for most of us. It's rarely cut and dried, and the boundaries shift all the time. We know that it's not good for our own mental health, or for those around us, if we are a control freak, but at the same time sometimes we have to step up and say, 'This is on me.' One way of doing that is to recognise if your inner voice is being stifled by the loud opinions of others. I think if you really listen, you will always find it eventually. Then you just have to make yourself heard.

Control is such a complicated, loaded word. We teach our children self-control as they grow because it's essential for them to be able to live in the world, to make friends and not be selfish. As humans, with our deeply rooted 'tribe' mentality, society and the expectations of others exerts a huge amount of control over us. And how that is dictated to us depends on who we are and the attitudes in society at the time, whether it's little girls being told they must always be ladylike and not get dirty, or little boys being discouraged from playing with toys that 'aren't for them'. If we grow up with relationships that are difficult or fractured, or even damaging, then it often manifests in us as adults in how we allow others to control us, or how we try to control them.

Like so many things, achieving the right level of control in our lives comes down to confidence – the confidence to listen to ourselves and ensure that others are listening to our views too. And as we all know, confidence comes from within. It comes from knowing and accepting who we are, trusting ourselves and our own abilities, and being comfortable in our own skin. We cannot always control when we feel anger, guilt or shame, but we can accept that they are part of our experience and look at them in the light rather than hiding them away in the dark. Guilt and shame are toxic if we hold them inside. They can make us feel like we are not enough, even that we are not worthy of love. Like anger, they feel like ugly things we should hide. Judgement is a form of control that makes us change our behaviour for fear that love or respect will be taken away from us if we don't. But if we have the courage to confront these things and ask what is making us feel like that, or whose judgement have we internalised, we will find the power to let so much of it go. Because that is where true inner peace comes from, not from denying that the difficult, darker things exist.

RE-
CON-
ING

RECONNECTING

Ultimately, I've come to the conclusion that true inner beauty is rooted in being able to be present in our own minds and bodies. Without that, we become too focused on the next thing that's coming along, and we allow the busyness of our lives and the opinions of others to swamp us. When things are difficult, our instinct can be to rush around trying to fix everything that's wrong outside of us, and not give ourselves the space to address what's happening inside our own minds. To truly know ourselves, our beauty and our truth, we need to find a way to check back in.

One way to reconnect with ourselves is through laughter. Being able to laugh at ourselves injects this new energy which means we can play with what we're doing. We all feel vulnerable and exposed sometimes when we go out on a limb and try something we're unfamiliar with. So try to be like a kid, unselfconsciously exploring the world, and don't take it so seriously. Be light-hearted about it, ready to laugh and see the funny side if things don't go quite to plan. Without doubt, throughout my life laughter has always been the best medicine. It can rewire any situation you're in, even if you're feeling fed up and sad.

My husband makes me laugh all the time. He's the master of defusing situations by reminding us both of the funny side. If we're having a disagreement about something, he can derail me and send me into giggles by saying something, and before you know it, the issue doesn't seem quite so serious and we can resolve it with a more level head. It's a brilliant tool to have in your armoury as a parent too, to be able to defuse any situation and make somebody laugh, and it teaches your kids not to take life too seriously.

When somebody sits on *This Morning*'s sofa, the fact that they're about to be on live telly and this is a really unusual situation for them often makes them visibly nervous. They might also be talking about something that's very personal to them. Sometimes I just sit them down and tell them I'm there for them and that they have our total support – if anything goes wrong, we'll jump in. But if you can also make them laugh in that moment, you can see it in their face that their anxiety disappears.

Laughter is hugely contagious; if you see two people laughing, the chances are that you will start too before you even know what they're laughing about. It's like a yawn, isn't it? So, if you're having a bad day, if you're feeling very stressed about something or your anxiety is going through the roof, find something to make you laugh. Watch clips of your favourite comedian, or go on YouTube and watch something funny.

We post clips online from *This Morning* where things have gone horribly wrong, and they are watched by millions and millions of people. I get messages all the time saying, 'Oh my God, I haven't laughed all week and this made me howl!' Or, 'There's not been much to laugh about recently, but this was brilliant, this really helped.' I love that we

With all aspects of life, it's about finding that balance

might be the reason, in that one person's day, that helped them raise a smile and pulled them out of a bad moment.

Just being able to laugh at situations gives you a bit of perspective. It can help you step back from what's making you angry, anxious or stressed. It won't make the situation go away, but in the moment, it's a good tool to possess.

However, sometimes what we need in order to reconnect is silence. However difficult or unfamiliar it may feel at first, you need to practise sitting still for a while with your own thoughts. It's really important to learn the art of doing nothing, of just sitting there quietly within yourself, within your own being, with only your thoughts for companionship. It isn't something that comes overnight or happens very quickly and it can feel really uncomfortable, so don't feel like you've failed if you can't do it at first. It's a bit like a physical stretch – those that you find the most difficult are the ones you need to keep practising because that's where the muscles are tightest.

I think you've got to make a conscious choice to almost surrender yourself to it. You might say, 'Right, I'm going to do this for five minutes today, and tomorrow I'm going to do it for six minutes, and the next day I'm going to do it for seven minutes.' Try to go with it without overthinking the process. Just notice how you feel before and how you feel afterwards. This is certainly something I don't think we do enough because we are often so distracted. We don't check in enough with ourselves.

If you are a busy person, you might think you haven't got time to find that space or that stillness. You haven't got time to be bored, even if you want to. I would say that you need this more than ever, because as with all aspects of life, it's about finding that balance. If you can shut your eyes and go to a calm place you've created within yourself, no matter what else is happening at the time – whether you're at work, whether you're at home and your kids are driving you mad, or if you're just feeling a little bit anxious about something – then you've got that with you all the time. It's wholly yours. You don't need to buy anything, you don't need to go anywhere. It's in you. You've just got to close your eyes and find that space.

You know when it's snowed and you walk outside and the world's covered in white and everything sounds slightly different? It's all a bit more muffled and a bit quieter and everything's a bit more beautiful. That's how it feels to me. I close my eyes and I'm still in my world, but it's just got that soft blanket of fresh snow, making everything a bit more still and a bit more peaceful. The crisp fresh air brings me clarity.

I dismissed the idea of meditation for ages because the idea of finding time to sit and do nothing at any point during my day – let alone twice a day for 20 minutes! – felt like something that was never going to happen. But when I began to really focus on carving out space and time to look inward, I decided I was going to give it a go, and now I really wish I had found it sooner.

I think there's a misconception that you have to be able to totally clear your mind, to still everything that is going on in there, to be able to meditate. But that's actually not the case at all. In fact, it's important that you don't put too much expectation on yourself, otherwise it just becomes another area in which we think we have to be perfect. Actually, you just have to surrender to it and accept what comes. This is definitely one of the reasons why it has been good for me as I overthink things all the time, which can lead me to try to control things. Sometimes meditation for me is uplifting and revitalising and all those lovely things you want it to be, but there have been times when it hasn't felt good at all. But that's an important lesson – what will be, will be.

I took a course with Will Williams, who has written a book about the meditation he teaches called *The Effortless*

Mind. He explains that the speed of modern-day life is too fast for our biology, for our brains to cope with, and we respond by going into autopilot and relying more on our inherent fight-or-flight mechanism, which gets us through the day but inhibits the bit of our brain where our creative functions come from. His form of meditation is mantra-based, which means that you repeat a phrase in your mind. This really works for me, as it means that whenever I feel my thoughts moving away too much, I can come back to the mantra. There are other forms of meditation; you have to find the one that works for you.

Meditation calms down the fear centre of the brain that tries to keep the plates spinning to get you through the day. This gives you space to reconnect and allows you to think more clearly. I've definitely found that the time I spend meditating is worth it, as somehow it makes me more efficient, calmer, and means I make better decisions. What I love about meditation, now that I have been practising it for a while, is that it almost does the work for you. I usually just need to show up, close my eyes and say my mantra, and I feel like my body somehow takes over and knows what to do. I have this sense that it is connecting up cells in my brain and repairing some of the chaos that is in there. I think it's similar to the way in which talking therapies can help you refile or process some of the things in your brain, which is why all these things work really well together. There's probably not one magic key that will allow you to reconnect to yourself, if this is something you need to do, but all these things are tools in the toolkit – you just have to find what works for you.

If you are struggling to sit with your thoughts and do nothing, then you could start by writing. Sit down somewhere quiet, where you can be alone, and just write what's in your head. Write it all out and don't hold back, don't hide anything from yourself. If you don't want anyone to see it, then put it in a diary, or even burn the pages! But just write and write and write. You might think, 'Yeah, but it's not going to help, it's not going to change anything.' Well, often it's not about 'solving' what's in your head. You're not trying to find a magic wand that will instantly and magically put right whatever is wrong. Sometimes it's just about finding a different perspective, giving it an outlet, a way to be heard and released. Writing about your problems can turn the noise down in your head. It can release the pressure, if only temporarily.

Even once we recognise the need to create time for ourselves, when life is busy it can feel so hard to do this. And particularly in the early stages, when it perhaps feels uncomfortable to sit still with your thoughts. Ask yourself this question, and be truthful with the answer: when you're looking at your day, all those things that you're juggling, are they all absolutely necessary or adding pleasure to your life? Or are you adding pressure to your life? If you took something away, what difference would it make? Are you taking away pressure or pleasure? I bet you there are a few things in your life that you could shift.

I like that I'm having conversations with myself and rediscovering myself, but at the same time I'm conscious that I don't want to fall into the trap of overanalysing, which I know I have a tendency to do. It's possible to replace a feeling of detachment with so much introspection that it stops you being present in the moment and actually living. The irony!

Apart from stilling my racing mind and helping me sleep, there are other practical, everyday ways in which learning to be more present has helped me. One is that I make sure I appreciate the small things in life, particularly the little rituals. I take time to make my coffee in the morning, enjoying how it smells, looking forward to the first sip. Sometimes when I wake up, I light a candle. I try to find joy in everything I do. So, when I'm making the dinner, rather than focusing on all the other things I have to do and thinking, 'Oh my God, I've got to cook, I haven't got time for this!', I try to consciously think, 'Right. Now I'm going to make a meal for my husband and my children and I like cooking so I'm going to enjoy this, I'm going to focus on it. I'm going to put my love and care into it and not worry about anything else while I concentrate on this.' It's not always that easy, of course, and I don't beat myself up about it if I fail sometimes, but bringing focus to these small rituals rather than seeing everything as a tick on your to-do list really works; it's about doing your best to be wholeheartedly present while performing them, rather than rushing through each item to get to the next thing you want to do.

I think this has a wider implication, too. When you give your complete focus to the small things, it not only stops you falling into the trap of believing that multitasking is a woman's best skill, that it should be celebrated, it's also a good starting point to truly ground you in the present. I now take so much pleasure in just looking up at the beauty of the moon, in valuing nature, and noticing the changing of the seasons. I am grateful for the opportunity to walk through Richmond Park with my family, watching the squirrels run around. To teach my daughter how to wash her hair. Just seeing these moments for what they are is what life's really all about. I think we all know that, deep down, but it's hard to remember sometimes when our minds are racing and all we can think about is the ever-present to-do list.

A particular ritual I have discovered recently that really helps me is playing the singing bowls – essentially a special bowl that produces quite amazing sounds and vibrations. I decided I was going to have an open mind and try lots of different things, and so I went to a healer who played. The bowls emit this amazing sound at different frequencies that you can feel in your body, so even those who are not at all interested in alternative therapies tend to really respond to the experience. Our bodies are 60 per cent water, and sound waves travel more quickly through liquids, so when a sound wave hits us we resonate with that. It's a wonderful feeling.

One of the things I love about playing the bowls at home is that it makes me slow down – the ones I play are crystal and delicate, so even just getting them out of their bags makes me focus and pay attention. Like any ritual, it sends a signal that I'm giving myself some time to listen to myself and what my mind and my body need at that moment.

The bowls are just one tool I use to carve out time for myself. I have become much better at balancing looking after others with looking after myself. For a long time I wasn't doing this – I didn't even think much about it, I knew I could cope with anything. I was this strong, resilient woman who didn't really need that much, and as long as everybody else was happy, then I was absolutely fine, too. But the problem is that you forget to check in with yourself and see who you are, and suddenly you are addicted to the overwhelm, adrift from your own needs and detached.

So yes, we're capable of doing everything and we *can* cope, but that doesn't mean we should. My new superpower is looking after both myself and other people – balancing and marrying the two so they run alongside each other. It's important not to feel guilty about this because one enhances the other. I'm better at looking after everybody else because my head's in a much better place.

Apart from meditation, another really good way to be still and be with yourself is to start connecting with anything that is natural. The sun, moon and stars are constants that have always been there and remain the same. Something as simple as going for a walk, putting my hands on my belly and just breathing in and out, slowing everything down, really helps me to feel connected to nature, which, in turn, calms me. As I breathe, I try to consciously think, 'Right, what can I do to slow my heart rate down?' I like to focus on those things around me that are fundamental, that aren't created or manufactured, that are just there.

I feel a deep connection with the moon. I am drawn to it because it's been seen as a feminine symbol for thousands of years by many people far wiser and more connected to the earth than me. The moon is my anchor when I need to focus and take a few breaths. There is something comforting in the solid mass, lit up with its reflected light, looking back at you. Then there is the fact that it's there at night, when the world is quieter (although the brain can be noisier) and it's easier to find that silence we all need. All those interferences and influences from the world – your kids, your job, your phone, the boxset you're into – are gone for now. The moon's arrival tends to bring with it peace, and with that comes your thinking time, your space. It's partly why the moon has become important to me, because it represents *my* time. I can take a few deep breaths. I look. I listen. I open my mind and my ears to myself. These nocturnal moments are a meditation, of sorts.

The moon has a unique energy that I tap into, both on the mental and the physical side. My menstrual cycle is synced with the full moon, which, as a woman, feels like old magic to me! I don't know how it does it. Also, if you are with a group of girls, your cycles can sync up. I work with Patsy, who does my make-up, and Ciler, who does my hair, and my sister is at my house an awful lot, so we're together all the time, and we are all in sync. There is something that bonds people who menstruate on that level. It really does feel like magic.

Perhaps another reason I identify with the moon is that our view of it changes every day. And, oh my God, I change so much, day to day. Whether that's mood swings, how I see things, how I feel, how I view the world. And I think that's common. We're allowed to change. We are not fixed beings; we are not stuck on this one path. We can make choices, decisions, we can mess up and make mistakes. That's all OK. We learn and grow from mistakes. And it's so important to do that, and to know that you can do that. You are capable of it and you have permission. Everybody else is making mistakes too. You don't have to hide it.

I do think we lose sight of nature and the natural, and I think that bringing those things back into your life helps you. People call it grounding; you stand outside, put your feet on the grass, feel the earth; you sit down, feel it beneath your tailbone, feel that connection with Mother Earth. There is a calmness in grounding that I find attractive, because life is so, so busy. When we went into lockdown in spring 2020, everybody stood still and nature flourished. I think that is a really good image of what taking these moments for yourself should be like. Look inward, be still, have some time to yourself and see how quickly things begin to change and flourish. Ask yourself: what do I need right now?

The real beauty of being able to reconnect to ourselves and how we really feel, to sit with ourselves in the present moment, is that we can take comfort in the fact that everything we feel or experience or go through will pass. The only real emotion, the only reality that we have is the present, that thing that we feel right this moment, right now. Anything else that we're holding on to is either a memory, a conditioned way of being, or the fear of a future we cannot control. When we look at it like this, we can start to let go of so many of the difficult and unhelpful thoughts and feelings that we're clinging to. We can realise that we aren't presently feeling so many of those things and, as we sit there, we are in fact simply holding onto a memory of them. We can then start to calmly sort through and decide which memories serve us well – those times we overcame and did something we had doubted we could, for example – and let go of those that have no purpose at all.

As you do that, give yourself permission to just feel who you are today. What do you need today? Maybe today's the day that you will say to yourself, 'I love you just as you are'. If you are not ready, then that's OK. It will come. And if you feel a bit sad, that's OK too. If you don't feel like having a laugh or smiling, if you don't feel like getting out of bed, that's fine. That's what you need right now, right here, in this moment. Everything you have and need is right here. Just as you are. In this moment you are everything.

We already have everything we need. Mother Nature is very clever at providing us with that. In nature, everything lives in balance, surrounded by exactly what it needs in order to survive and thrive. And we're the same. If we are honest with ourselves and we are living our life to our own heartbeat and not somebody else's, then we will see that we have everything we need to thrive and survive right here. We are all beautiful and wise in our own unique way, we just have to give ourselves the space to recognise and understand that.

Be kind to yourself. Tune in to yourself. Only you know what you need today.

INTUITION

It's ironic for me to be writing this here, but I think it's important that we stop believing we will find the one person, book or podcast that will unlock everything for us. Of course we can look to others for elements of wisdom or advice, but the reality is that we know ourselves better than anyone. We know what we need. We know how we feel. We just need to find a way to hear it. Another way to do this is to connect with our intuition – our inner voice.

If you are overwhelmed, detached and chasing your tail, you're going to find it hard to tap into your intuition. Other people's opinions, advice or feedback will cloud your awareness and block your way. You're not going to be able to see the way through. So how do you start listening to your intuition? How do you switch it on? You have to clear the path.

Unless I actively make sure that I give myself time and space to reconnect and be calm, my mind runs away and jumps from thing to thing, looking three steps ahead. It is very, very busy. But this means I'm not present or engaged in that moment, and in order to hear your intuition, you need to be totally engaged and present. So I try to slow things down and pull myself back into my body, back into this moment in time, to anchor myself and root myself to the spot and turn my intention inward. I try to do a scan through my body to see how I physically feel from head to toe, rather than putting all my attention into my conscious thoughts and trying to work out what might be behind them.

Slow things down and pull myself back into my body... into this moment in time

I'm coming to rely on my intuition more because I'm learning there's more clarity in my heart and gut than there is in my head. We often overintellectualise our feelings; we try to argue or problem-solve our way out of them when the answer is in the body all along. My gut is easier to control than my head. It feels more stable somehow. My head still runs around, though. Life is busy. Regardless of how much I want to sit still and play my bowls, meditate or look at the moon, life continues and there's no getting away from the fact that I'm a mum of three and it is busy. I wouldn't have it any other way.

Sometimes, when I've been stuck in a position where I don't know what to do or think, when I've found it really hard to come to a decision, I've tried to force a result or an answer because I just want it to be done. I want to stop thinking about it. But nine times out of ten, that's when I've made a mistake or gone for the wrong option. I knew on some level that it wasn't quite right and that I was forcing the situation. Alternatively, I have asked advice from so many different people that I have ended up doing what they would do in that situation and not what I should do. It's good to get advice, but that's all it is. You're in charge of your destiny, no one else.

Sometimes you have to be patient enough to ask questions of yourself and trust that the answers will come. Find that space in your own head and sit with your question. Be prepared to wait and not rush yourself. And then make those important decisions when there is clarity. Slow things down and tune out all the external influences that are blocking your path and your intuition will take over. It will come.

The most profound lesson I learned about trusting my intuition came when I gave birth for the first time. I felt so lucky that my body knew how to make and grow a baby. When I went into labour with Harry, I woke up in the night and my waters had broken. When I got to hospital, the midwife told me I was fully dilated and ready to push. But like many first-time mums, I was scared. I wanted to have an epidural because I wanted some sort of control and I was afraid the pain would get in the way of that.

So I had the epidural and it slowed the birth down and I ended up having a forceps delivery. I didn't have a bad birth experience, and perhaps at the time the epidural was the right thing to do. But with hindsight, I can't help thinking that I let fear get in the way. All the signals were there that my body knew exactly what it was doing; I simply had to trust it to push this baby out so I could hold it in my arms. Had I been less scared I think my intuition would have told me that.

After Harry was born, like so many new mothers, I allowed too many external influences to intrude, telling me what I was supposed to be doing, drowning out my intuition which actually knew so much more than I gave it credit for. Don't get me wrong, a lot of the advice I was given was very useful. But I still think my judgement became clouded at times, both from the overwhelming amount of information out there and my fear that I would get it wrong and not be the perfect mother. I didn't trust in myself and so I made decisions that – deep down – I wanted to do differently but was too scared to in case I was judged as being wrong.

By the time I had Chester, my third and largest baby, I had so much more confidence in myself and my intuition. I knew how to identify the advice that was useful and drown out the external noise that wasn't. Chester was in the back-to-back position, which can be trickier and more painful, but I gave birth to him in water and I experienced the amazing power of what my body was able to do.

Becoming a mum for the first time is definitely a real test of our intuition. But what I came to understand is that for a child, the most important thing is that they feel loved. That they feel safe. That they feel nurtured. That they can trust you. The more I tapped into that, the more I felt safe and comfortable within myself. I just had to listen to and trust my intuition. And it's not just parenting where this is true – there are lots of times in our lives when our intuition can be undermined; you just need to find a way to create space around yourself so that you can listen to your own guidance about what is right.

Kids are really closely in touch with their intuition. Before they receive all the information from the adult world they just go with how they feel. For example, they might be nervous about their first day at school and we'll tell them not to worry and that it'll all be fine. But their intuition is spot on; it *is* a scary moment. We don't want them to be afraid, and our developed, rational minds know that they are not in any danger. We have to do this, but it still makes me feel sad, as we essentially knock back those innate gut feelings they have and start papering over them. We tell them not to listen to their intuition and to listen to us instead.

When we stop listening to our intuition, I think that's what stops us opening our minds and recognising what can truly help us. I know that crystals really help me. My parents always had a piece of quartz hanging in their lounge and I was always mesmerised by it when I was a kid. I carry a piece of smoky quartz whenever I'm filming. It's said to be calming and to protect you from negative energy. I can't tell you in an intellectual way why this was good for me, but my intuition tells me that it helped. So often we feel something instinctively in our body, but our inner critic shouts us down and tells us to ignore it. But if we learn to reconnect with our intuition it will show us the difference between what we think we want and what we actually need.

We often explain intuition by saying, 'I just felt it; I just had this really clear feeling.' I think we've all had those moments of 'I just knew.' 'I just knew it was wrong,' or 'I just knew I had to go,' or 'I just knew I had to answer the phone at that point.' Those are real moments of clarity – that initial spark and the immediate feeling. Sometimes some of our biggest life decisions are made in an instant. And if you come to know and recognise that feeling of absolute intuition, you will also know when it's not there, when you are making decisions based on what other people might think, or from a place of fear.

I think one of the biggest decisions you can make is making the decision to get married. When the time comes you've probably been in the relationship for a while, but when somebody actually asks you that question, 'Will you marry me?', you don't have very long to give a reply. So, you are almost forced to make this real gut decision that is going to set out your life forever. And that's why everybody says, 'When you know, you know.' I think proposals are the perfect example of this. I wish every decision was the same!

So how do you start listening to your intuition? You have to clear the pathway and get rid of that racing mind I spoke about earlier. Always try to remember your first gut instinct when facing a decision, even if you explore other options afterwards. What was your initial response when you realised you would have to make a choice about something? Write it down if you need to, so you don't forget it, and then consider all the other options, listen to advice, think about how you'd feel if you went with each one. Then come back to that instinctive response. How do you feel about it now? Ask yourself, is this what I want? Is this what I need? Is this what is good for me right now? Or am I just clouding my judgement with what everybody else needs me to do? Look for the physical signs as well. Are you getting shivers? Are you getting butterflies? Are you getting a tummy ache? Your body gives you these signals and the more you tune into them, the easier they are to spot and the more attuned you become to yourself.

Something that gets in the way of intuition is judgement and knowledge. There's the fear of being judged by others, of course, but there is also our judgement of other people, which we can sometimes confuse with instinct. If somebody comes up to us in the street and we don't know who they are, we need to make a very quick call as to whether or not we feel safe with that person, if the situation carries any kind of risk. Our intuition is part of this, but fear can also knock intuition on the head. Although that might feel like a gut reaction, it may actually be controlled by past traumatic experiences – so you are telling yourself that something is dangerous when actually, if you listened to yourself more carefully, you would realise that there is nothing to be scared of and you just need to take control.

Both judgement and instinct are influenced by our own life experiences. So two people can view the same situation from completely different angles, depending on what's happened to them. If we've had a difficult or frightening experience in the past, then this can have a big impact on how our minds and bodies behave in situations that we perceive as similar to that upsetting event, even if in reality they are not. Your body is trying to protect you by taking into account its learned experience, but this is not always helpful. In severe cases, we need to seek professional help so we can deal with these things and hopefully stop them from affecting us and clouding our intuition. But even if you haven't experienced serious trauma, it's worth thinking about how your past impacts your perception of the present.

Another reason to recognise the emotional baggage that we all lug around with us is to aid empathy. If you know that you react – or overreact sometimes – to things based on your own life experiences, then you can understand that other people will do that too. How others approach things and where they come from will be influenced by things that have happened to them.

EMBRACING
INDIVIDUALITY

It sometimes feels as though figuring out who you are and what you want is the work of a lifetime. You have to somehow filter out all the other influences, all the pressures that come from society telling you what you should be, so you can hear your own voice. And then, of course, you have to find the confidence to live that truth out in the world, risking judgement from others. So it's no wonder that sometimes it feels easier to retreat and not try to express your true individual self. I know I have done this in different ways in different times in my life.

When I was a kid, I was very shy, believe it or not. Loads of my schoolfriends are amazed at what I've gone on to do for a living because I was the kid that had my sleeve pulled right down and my hand in front of my face. I would talk into my sleeve and not look anybody in the eye properly. I didn't have much confidence and I was terrified of not fitting in, of saying anything that my friends might think was not funny or cool. My worst nightmare was to stand out in any way; it felt so much safer just to blend in with the crowd. I didn't think about my own identity because I just wanted to be one of the herd.

I think many children and teenagers feel like this at some point. After all, humans have a tribe mentality that makes us want to belong on a very basic level. There's a security that comes with fitting in. But if conformity continues into adulthood it can be a problem. By sticking with the herd-like mentality, you won't express yourself in a way that is totally honest. If you feel like you have to do the things everybody else is doing, then you're probably missing out on the opportunity to explore what you are best at. If you're afraid to stand out from the crowd, you may not discover your superpowers, your unique skills, and you'll be holding yourself back.

Even if we grow past that playground herd mentality when we become adults, many of us still have a nagging feeling that something's missing and something's lacking. In the back of our mind we know we've coasted for a long time and played it safe for fear of looking silly or being judged. And guess what? The thing that's missing is you. It's your individuality and all of those things that make you 'you'.

This is when being a little bit scared, showing a little vulnerability and dipping a toe in the water is the only answer. You've got to be brave and tell that child within you that you can't seek safety in the herd anymore. Try those things that you've always wanted to do, and if you fail, it doesn't matter. It's OK to get it wrong – in fact, often the fear of getting it wrong is worse than the feeling when it actually happens. If you do mess up somehow, it's almost never the drama you think it's going to be. And let's face it, what's the other option? Not trying at all?

A really good example of this for me was when I started doing some modelling while I was still at school. I'd been spotted at The Clothes Show, which was a huge fashion event at the time. Part of me wanted to run away and hide but there was also another part of me that saw what an amazing opportunity this was and something in me told me to try out. In order to get jobs, I had to go to casting auditions, which were completely the opposite of staying comfortably within the herd – you had to stand out, and you had to do it while loads of people you didn't know were staring at you.

Just before I walked in, if I was auditioning for a commercial, for example, I might be given a script. It was like what we now see on *X Factor* – you'd go in and stand there in front of a table of people, say your name and a little bit about yourself, and then you'd read some of the script. Speaking out loud in front of people I didn't know was literally my idea of hell, and I'd rather have been anywhere else. The first few times I did it I was utterly useless, and it just fed into my insecurities that I wasn't cut out for it.

In the waiting room outside, other girls would come in, see somebody they knew and they'd be chatting and laughing, while I was looking over, thinking, 'Oh my God, they're so confident with each other. I'm just a different breed. I'm a different type of person. I don't have that. I'm not capable of being that way.' The more confidence they had, the more mine would disappear and the more insecure I'd become.

So I had to make a decision: was I just going to give up and say, 'Well, maybe this just isn't for me,' or was I going to decide, 'Actually, I'm going to make myself do this'? I was doing something I really enjoyed and, in my heart,

I didn't want to stop. I knew I had to keep trying. I think you can practise confidence and doing things you don't necessarily feel naturally comfortable with. If something's holding you back, if fear is getting in the way of something you really want for yourself, then you've just got to almost pretend for a bit, until it becomes easier.

So I kept doing it. I put myself in those uncomfortable situations and forced myself to look people in the eye and talk. In order to find my confidence, to be true to what I really wanted, I had to accept the fact that it might all go horribly wrong – I might forget my words, look or sound ridiculous, or nobody would laugh at a joke I cracked – and just do it anyway. And it worked. And each time I was booked to do something, my confidence was boosted a little more because I knew I'd been chosen, so therefore somebody had believed in me. Whenever you put yourself in the position of being judged by somebody, where somebody might make a decision on you, it's a really scary place to be. However, the more you do it the less scary it becomes.

Doing kids' telly gave me a lot more confidence on this front. I learned that we could play around a bit, maybe go a little off-script, come away from the autocue and make a joke. When it worked it increased my self-belief. And when it didn't, I realised that it didn't matter as much as I thought it would. My increased confidence meant I didn't shrivel up if something went wrong, if I tripped over my words or made a mistake on the autocue. It was the biggest learning curve to realise that it just didn't *matter*. When you learn to be OK with your mistakes then everybody just laughs along with you when you mess up.

I now have a really high embarrassment threshold. I've made so many mistakes in my life – they just seem to follow me around! That's never going to change, so now I totally forgive myself if I slip up and get something wrong. Yet at the same time, I think I probably had to learn not to mind early on due to my dyslexia. I can't spell or read out loud very well, so I often got things wrong in class. As a kid, the idea of anybody laughing at me would cripple me inside, and I actively avoided any situations where this might happen. On *This Morning* I misread or mispronounce words from the autocue all the time and it makes us crumble with laughter. One of my favourites was my struggle with 'shiitake mushroom'. You can probably guess where I went wrong here (if not... google it!) – hilarious! In many ways, we actually live for these moments. When everything's perfect and goes according to plan, then that's great, but it's when things go wrong that the magic happens.

To give yourself permission to laugh at yourself is to give yourself permission not to be perfect. And that's really powerful. Subconsciously, we have this drive to be 'perfect', as if this will solve all of life's problems, when so often it's what causes them in the first place. If you're not holding yourself to such a high standard of perfection, then you can see the funny side if something goes wrong, and even enjoy it. Fear of embarrassment stops us doing lots of things, but the best way around this is just to learn to laugh at yourself, and not to mind if you slip up.

I have accepted that I am never going to be the most articulate person, and I'm never going to be able to spell or read perfectly. But that doesn't mean I can't communicate and make people understand what I have to say. Writing this book has been such a challenge, but with a lot of time and perseverance, I pushed myself and found a way to, somehow, get all of these words on the page. The way I speak and write is similar in tone to having a conversation with your friend in the pub and – guess what – they are the best conversations! The ones you really want to have.

You can't control everything. Trying to be perfect is like having a stone hanging around our necks. People get things wrong, and this is often funny. If you can laugh at yourself, then you can accept that what makes us human is our mistakes. It means you are not taking it all too seriously, which is important because things you take too seriously have too much power and control over you. If you take things more lightly, you get some of that power back.

And also, laughing feels so good! We know how great it is to really belly laugh and feel all the endorphins, those feel-good chemicals, being released. Our greatest stories from growing up, from being with our friends, are the ones where something funny happened. We hold on to those memories for a reason, because laughter makes us feel really good.

On *This Morning*, we once had a guest who did laughter therapy. She told us that your body doesn't know the difference between real and fake laughter – you can enjoy the feel-good hormones from both. Give it a go! If you feel stressed or anxious, put your hands on your stomach and start laughing as loudly as you can. See what happens! You might find it gives you the giggles, and suddenly you are really laughing and everything feels a bit better.

I think social media also has an impact on how much people are able to be themselves. People often ask me about how it impacts my life because so many people have an opinion on what I do, my image and my children. But though this might sound like a strange thing to say, I'm honestly OK with it. It's not like I block out everyone else's opinions and only listen to my own. I do listen and hear. But the important thing is to know whose opinions you value and only let those in.

The opinions of people I really love and admire are the ones I hold on to, that are really helpful to me. But even then, I think you have to have the strength to know your own mind, as just because someone loves you and knows you really well, doesn't mean they are going to be right 100 per cent of the time. Sometimes my mum, who I adore more than anybody in the world and whose opinions I respect so much, will occasionally say, 'I wasn't sure about that dress you wore today. That wasn't very you.' Thanks, Mum! Yet while I want my mum to like what I'm wearing – I respect her opinion and she's got really good taste! – it's OK for people to have differing opinions. Did I like it? Yes. So I'll just tell her that. I don't need to change how I dress for anybody, as long as I feel good in it. (Don't get me wrong, she says lots of lovely things too.)

As humans, we thrive in communities. So other people's opinions do affect us. But it's important to remember that we can't please everybody, so there's no point in even trying. It's much easier to decide what you like and what you don't like yourself, rather than trying to dress or behave in certain ways for other people. Because you just get tied up in knots and it's exhausting; it just doesn't work. If you really know how you feel about something, when somebody says, 'I don't think you should do that,' or, 'I'm not sure you should have behaved like that,' you can honestly lay your hand on your heart and reply, 'I did this for these reasons and it was right for me.' It's not always easy but that's you being your truest self. And knowing you are doing that is a powerful weapon against self-doubt: 'I have to do it like this because I know that is what's right for me.'

So that's why living my life in the glare of the media – both social and otherwise – doesn't affect me too much. However, I do still think that social media is an area where we need to take great care. It's good to be inspired by what other people post, for sure. And social media can be a great tool for learning. But the danger is that we have taken the ethos of a brand that was invented by marketing and advertising companies and have turned it on ourselves as individuals. There is a pressure to use social media to project our own 'personal brand' without necessarily being completely and utterly true to the person behind it. And if you have created a brand, rather than expressing your true self, then you have to continue to play the role that fits that, which affects how you behave and think about yourself. You have to start living this completely different role. Wearing outfits you're not even sure you like because they fit with what you want to project, or doing your hair in the way that suits the character you've put out there. Change is good; you can and should change. But you should grow and develop in a way that is honest and true, rather than projecting something unreal that represents how you want to be seen. Believe in yourself, rather than a social media persona that you've created.

I was talking to my daughter about identity. She's nine, and already she thinks about her own identity and who she is. She draws comparisons between her and her friends – perhaps some are better at maths or sport – and already she feels inferior because she senses other people are enjoying successes around her. And social media magnifies that feeling beyond our immediate world. We look at other people and nine times out of ten it makes us feel worse about ourselves. Yet we are drawn to it. We think that if only we had what they've got, or learn to do our eyeliner like they do in their pictures, we'll feel better about ourselves. Instead of thinking, 'OK, that's their

I knew they affected lots of other people too. I knew then that I was going to ask them in a way that made sense to me. So many of the people watching would be people like me: interested in a broad range of different things but not necessarily buying into the political vocabulary you get on serious current affairs shows. That's not what they wanted from me, so I thought, I'm just going to ask my questions as if I'm speaking to my mum or a friend.

It proved to me that I can interview different people from different backgrounds and professions and I don't have to change in any way. If I remain true to myself, whether I am interviewing the prime minister or a reality star, then it will be better because it comes from a place that is authentic. It's such a great piece of advice that I wish I could have told it to myself years ago: don't adapt what you're doing for other people because you think that's what they're expecting from you. Be consistently 'you' in all situations.

Now that I've found this confidence and strength in my own voice, I want to make sure I consistently speak my truth – but always with love and empathy. There's a big difference between this and 'telling it how it is', which is not what I do. Telling someone 'how it is' is often done in an aggressive way without taking into account the other person's thoughts and feelings, whereas I think that, as humans, we have to have understanding and empathy for what that other person is going through. So I will speak my truth – what's in my mind and in my heart – but always with love and an awareness of those around me. If it comes from that place and it's true for me but others are critical of it, then I can let go of any responsibility for how they feel. I'm not going to hold their anger for them. If it's something that is true and honest and I communicate it with empathy and it still sparks anger within someone, then they need to do their own work.

Have compassion: compassion for yourself, compassion for others. We all know how it feels to be judged, how that saps our confidence and makes us scared to embrace who we really are. So don't be judgemental. You never really know what's going on in someone's life. So many times we read stories about people and the events seem so shocking and terrible and awful, only for more details to come out years later and you think, 'Wow, is that what really happened? Oh my God, if only we'd known that.' How can you judge something if you don't have the full story in front of you? And nobody has the full story in front of them, unless you are that person, living in their head, in their mind. The only full story you have is your own, and that's the story you need to read, and that's the story you need to get to know. No one else's.

Women are often taught to be modest. We absorb the idea that talking about our good qualities and celebrating our achievements is showing off. This is another barrier to discovering and understanding the things that make you uniquely you. We all have different superpowers, we just need to work out what they are. They don't have to be unusual achievements or skills. You don't need to be a concert pianist or an Olympic athlete. What do you think your superpowers are? I'd encourage you to write them down, and then you can look at yourself from a different viewpoint on your low days.

'What are your superpowers?'

SUPERPOWERS

I thought I'd talk through some of the things that make me who I am, and things that I think are my superpowers in the hope that it inspires you to consider yours. These are the things that, when I tap into them, feel the most like 'me', like my best and truest self. Some people call this their highest self.

The first is empathy. I think that my daughter has this quality too and it's really rewarding to see it. The vast majority of people are empathetic to some degree. But I definitely feel a deep empathy for everyone and everything. The downside to this is that I cannot watch anything scary or upsetting because I take it on board so much that I feel like it is happening to me. If I'm speaking to somebody about something that was very painful for them, I have to remind myself that it's not my pain that I'm feeling, and I have to put up a little self-protection boundary; I have to hold on to my own energy and space because otherwise it can be utterly exhausting and depleting. But still, it's fundamental to who I am and, as I explained above, it's what helps me speak my truth in a way that is both authentic and kind.

Empathetic people are sometimes drawn towards other people's pain and suffering because they want to help and they want to heal, and sometimes that's at the expense of their own wellbeing. It helps me just to know this. When you can identify this about yourself then you can put things in place that help – and that doesn't mean making yourself a cold and uncaring person. I just make sure that

I protect myself slightly, so that I don't deplete myself too much. But the wonderful flipside is that I also really feed off people's positive energy in happier situations. And that's a lovely, intoxicating feeling.

I've learned to listen to understand, which is such an important skill. I like to sit and listen, and I like to hold space for people so that they can get things off their chest or discuss things and know that they are in a safe place. I try not to be a judgemental person. I try to understand that no matter what someone says, there must be a reason behind it. Even if it's not that obvious to me in the moment, and what they are saying seems shocking, it must come from somewhere. I'm not the oracle and I don't know everything, but I know I definitely have an ability to listen.

Another thing that makes me feel my higher self is inspiring and mentoring other people. I love that. It gives me a real buzz. Throughout my career, I've worked with people to help them get on their own path, then watched them grow and flourish. I get so much out of being in a position that allows me to give people opportunities and offer advice. If I can say something that helps somebody or puts them on the right track, I love that.

I think another of my superpowers is knowing that I am flawed and not being scared by that. I've learned that those cracks and breaks you inevitably pick up during the difficult times heal stronger, and the cement that glues them back together actually adds more to you as a person. It's as though a crack is made and there's a gap for learning to come in and fill it. So the more breaks and cracks there are, the more opportunity there is to fill them with life lessons. Your mind grows. You also learn to forgive yourself for those times when you may have judged things wrongly or behaved badly.

Expecting perfection of yourself and others is a road to nowhere. Once you understand that everybody is flawed in their own unique, beautiful way, that we're all learning, we're all doing our best and we're all trying, that gives you a humility, an understanding, and a much better outlook on life.

So there you go. These are my superpowers – the good things that came from stepping out of the herd, of growing my confidence, of making mistakes and learning to listen to my intuition. They are, I think, some of the best things that make me who I am. I am proud of them.

Now, what are your superpowers?

FEMINISM

I am a feminist. I believe, obviously, that men and women are completely equal. But sometimes I find myself worrying that I am not as good a feminist as I should be, or as I want to be. So much of what has changed for women in the last fifty or sixty years we owe to the feminists who campaigned, who gave up so much, who wouldn't sit down and be quiet in the face of scorn, disapproval and denial of their experiences. I am in awe of those women who struggled and put so much on the line so I can live the way I do. I don't want to ever take that for granted. But a problem arises when feminism becomes one more thing we think we have to be 'perfect' at, feeling guilty when we don't manage it. Sometimes I feel guilty that I have reaped the rewards from the hard work that these women have done and haven't given quite enough back yet. I look at the women who have done so much, are still making changes now, are campaigning and changing laws and I sometimes wonder whether I should be doing more. Now that my children are a little older, I have more time in my life and more space in my head to consider other issues that are important to me. Advocating for feminist issues is becoming more and more important to me.

Of course the irony is that part of the cause being fought by the women I look up to was for us not to have to measure up as the perfect woman to have a value. We are allowed to get things wrong sometimes. We are allowed to be exactly the type of woman we choose to be. Being a woman and a feminist includes the right to say, 'I'm a feminist and I support everyone's right to do as they choose, I can be an emotional feminist. I can be a feminist who likes to watch silly romcoms with her girlfriends. I can be a feminist who wants to put lipstick on. I can be a feminist who is house-proud. I can be a feminist who isn't ambitious. I can be a feminist if I don't want a career.'

Feminism is about *choice* – about being able to decide who you are and what you want. Traits such as empathy and emotional intelligence have traditionally been seen as feminine, whereas confidence and ambition, for example, have traditionally been seen as masculine. I don't think there is anything inherently male or female about any personality trait or emotion. But the pressures remain; many women still aren't comfortable being assertive because it's 'masculine' and many men worry that showing their emotions is somehow 'feminine'. I think it might be helpful for all genders to realise once and for all that emotions are fluid and aren't bound by gender. Some men need to draw more on their 'feminine' side too and learn to speak about their emotions and be more empathetic. I was shocked to discover that the leading cause of death in men under the age of 45 is suicide; learning to talk and ask for help is crucial to changing this. Women might benefit from taking on more stereotypically masculine traits, too. I think women might have mimicked 'male' traits in the past, understandably, because until very recently, success has looked like a man.

I am definitely a very emotional person; I feel deeply. Yet in order to succeed, even from a young age, you're told not to be too emotional, to be strong. Emotion is seen as a sign of weakness. Even now this still happens to me at work. People say, 'Holly is always crying on TV, it's so unprofessional.' The expectation is that a professional person would hold in their emotions, they would deny how they feel and they wouldn't cry at something. So, to be professional, you have to be unfeeling?

It goes back to the idea that in order to succeed in business you need to have traits that are stereotypically 'masculine'. I started to feel that in order to fit in and succeed, I would have to shave off those bits that made me, 'me' – the softness, the emotional side, the more traditionally 'feminine' qualities. I felt like so much of myself had to be chipped away to make me into an acceptable package. But when you think about it, this leaves us trying to balance other people's demands: if you don't show any emotion you're a hard-nosed bitch; but if you're too emotional you're clearly illogical, hysterical and losing the plot. I realised I was expected to function in this tightly policed middle ground; this acceptable place that other people could cope with. But I ended up feeling like this weird person who was neither one way nor the other, and I certainly wasn't being true to myself.

Feeling deeply does not make you weak. I think there has been a shift and people are starting to realise this now. I've certainly come to understand that in my job, where

I'm interviewing and speaking to people on TV all the time, my emotion is actually my strength. It gives me a deeper connection with the people that I'm talking to. It was a connection I feared before because I often felt too connected, but now I don't think that's a bad thing. I think understanding people and having empathy is really important. Crying on air might seem unprofessional to some, perhaps those who feel uncomfortable dealing with emotion. But it's not unprofessional to me. It's just how I feel in that moment. And I can't change it. I don't want to change it. Realising that this unique trait is actually beneficial has brought me so much confidence. Many of us spend a large chunk of our lives at work, so if we don't feel comfortable and confident in that department, then that's always going to prevent us from living a rich, fulfilled life.

The playing field for women at work has levelled noticeably, even over the course of my own career. In my experience, overt sexism in the workplace is on the downward trajectory, and at quite a pace as well. I make sure that I am paid fairly for my work, equal to what a man with my experience and skillset would be paid. I think and hope that it's pretty well established now that there must be parity across the board when it comes to what different genders earn within my industry. I know that within other industries that's not the case, but at least there's more regulation now so perhaps there's hope for the future.

However, I think the problems women are still grappling with are more under the surface and so harder to call out or legislate against. We're still limited by the pressures that we put on ourselves. For example, a man is apparently still more likely to ask for a pay rise or promotion, whereas I feel like a woman is more likely to stay where she is, grateful for the fact that she's there. Or if she asks for a promotion, she might be seen as *overly* ambitious. And if you're a working mother, in particular, it can be hard to overcome the feeling that it's best not to put your head above the parapet too much because tomorrow your kid might have a temperature and you might have to ask for time off, or you might have a school play to get to, so therefore it's probably best not to rock the boat. I'm sure some fathers think like this too. Women spend 77 per cent more time on childcare than men. They're often still the ones getting a PE kit ready or remembering to buy new shoes, in addition to working.

When I had my first child there was a real turning point in my career. Up to that point, people thought I was just this kid on Saturday morning telly – they used to send bizarrely childish things to me in the office, like pink T-shirts with unicorns – and then I got pregnant and had Harry and it was like, boom – because I'd given birth, I was suddenly seen. It was like, 'Oh right, she's grown up now because she's a mum.'

It was really weird as it happened almost overnight. Somehow I couldn't be seen as a woman, and particularly a career woman, before that. I was just seen as a child and I wasn't taken seriously at all, I don't think. Society seems to be obsessed with both infantilising and sexualising women, often at the same time, disturbingly. After I had kids, I found I was seen less as a 'little girl', at least. That said, women who don't have children reach a certain age and are suddenly labelled as spinsters. It doesn't seem like you can ever really win! We need to get to a point when the labels and the pigeonholes stop. We need to start living within our own boundaries, not within the parameters of opinions placed on us by others.

Women's roles have changed so much at work and in the family over the years. But then again, not so much. As I sit writing this, my husband is upstairs on a conference call. My kids are outside. I went into the kitchen to get myself a drink before I started to write and my son said, 'Mummy, can we play UNO?' When I said I had to work, I felt guilty, because I thought, well, I'm not really *working*. But then I thought, it's funny that I even question this, that I even consider that my work might not be as important as my husband's, or isn't real work. If I don't believe it myself, how is anyone else going to? Where does that self-doubt come from? Why don't I believe my work is important? It's vital to look at this, to help understand who you are, what you want and what outside forces might be influencing how you see yourself and the decisions you make.

SUCCESS

We live in a society that sets unreasonable goals that we find ourselves buying into, despite knowing on some level that they are not right for us. It often feels like we have to be the perfect wife, daughter, mother, aunt, friend, colleague. We have to be the perfect ball-breaker at work, the perfect lover in the bedroom. And it's impossible to live up to all of these expectations.

Trying to achieve the 'dream life' – money, power, popularity, external beauty – is driving us to the point of exhaustion. We're stressing and striving for all of those things. I don't need to do a survey or look at a YouGov poll to know that anxiety and stress are on the up. Everybody's anxious and everybody's stressed and everybody's exhausted. That's the collateral damage of striving for perfection.

There are so many unhelpful stereotypes that can fall on us, particularly as women, that lead us to overwork ourselves. If we are working mums, we want to go into work and be the best we can be. Then we come home and we want to be the best mother we can be. There are so many pressures in all areas of our lives and they so easily become overwhelming. You end up spreading yourself too thin. You become a fragmented person, with a little bit of you at work, a little bit of you at home. You end up not being your best self because you're so exhausted and you're functioning on adrenaline, which isn't the best place from which to make decisions. It's another thing that leads us to detach, to be unable to listen to our inner voice. So how can we make things calmer and smoother?

How do we get to a place where we are managing our lives without all these external pressures making us unhappy, and learn to say no to things that aren't as important? How do we decide what actually is important?

The more I speak to people over the years, the more I come to realise that a lot of these imposed standards of so-called success are actually little to do with how any of us really feel inside. We feel we have to project this image of tranquil perfection, as though everything is really effortless. But actually, even those of us who look really together on the outside are struggling in some way.

Most of us know that what we see of other people's lives is not the whole story; we don't know what's going on below the surface. Yet it's still hard not to compare ourselves to others, to look at what someone else has, what they're doing, their clothes, their appearance, and assume it's all perfect and that they have it better than us. The problem is, instead of this triggering a feeling of happiness and joy inside us for them, comparison can hold a mirror up to our own insecurities and what we feel we're lacking. This shows itself as jealousy or envy, and these are not attractive qualities. We almost never admit to feeling like this, and yet the truth is that we possess these emotions and sometimes feel them about our closest friends, our own sisters, maybe even our own daughters. Like all emotions, jealousy is part of the tapestry that makes us 'us' and it's not going away; you can't just switch emotions off, so we need to look at them and ask some questions.

When I see somebody do something amazing that makes me think, 'Ah, I would love to do that,' then I feel envious. So the way that I've come to resolve this in my own head is to understand what I'm actually seeing is an example of possibility. That what that person has is just showing me that it *can* happen, and that it's out there for the taking. There's not a limited quota of beach holidays, so my friend having an amazing time in Greece doesn't mean I can never go. Promotions happen to more than one person, so someone else's work success doesn't take anything away from mine. It's shown me it's possible. It has inspired me.

Rather than letting these things trigger your insecurities, take a breath and remind yourself that there is enough for everybody. There is opportunity out there and this includes opportunities for you, too – you've just got to find them. Rather than destroying yourself because you feel insecure about other people's success, you will be taking yourself closer to your dream, rather than drifting on a tide of negativity further away from it. So, repackaged as possibility, jealousy might show you what you can achieve, if that's what you really want. But first you have to decide, do you really want it, or do you just want it because somebody else has got it? Once you've answered this question honestly, then you can deal with those feelings better.

If you look at things that you feel jealous or envious of, what would need to happen to make you feel better about that situation? So, for example, you see a picture on Instagram of your best friend who's just lost two stone and they look incredible. But instead feeling happy you actually find yourself feeling jealous. You're envious they managed to do that and it makes you feel insecure about your own body. So now think about this: if you could wave a magic wand and tomorrow they posted a picture where they'd put the weight back on would that make you feel better? Is the real issue that this has inadvertently reinforced some unexamined belief you have that you are in some way less valuable if you are heavier?

What if you were single and your best friend just started dating someone and they were blissfully happy. What would have to happen to stop you feeling jealous of that situation? Say they break up and he runs off with somebody else. You'd stop feeling jealous then – instead you'd feel sadness for your heartbroken friend – but actually what you've done is reminded yourself that relationships can look happy one minute and be destroyed in the next breath. So, as you console your friend, you might ask yourself, what's the point? That love is rubbish? What do you gain by following that train of thought rather than asking yourself why you feel envious in that situation?

Instead, ask: 'Why is this making me feel like this? Is it because I'm lonely? Is it because I really would love to meet somebody?' And then think about what you can do in order to change that situation. How did your friend meet their new partner? You can see with your own eyes now that it's possible to find an exciting new relationship, so how are you going to create that situation for yourself?

It's funny because if you change your mindset to be a little more accepting, a little more positive, a little lighter; if you count your blessings instead of feeling envious of others, you'll be pleasantly surprised by what you draw towards you. Because giving off that sort of positive, generous, altruistic energy is magnetising. Just put it out there and see what happens.

Letting go of jealousy and envy allows us to create much richer relationships with the women in our lives. If you accept your differences and similarities; if you remember that you don't have to have the same job, the same hair, the same weight, the same clothes, you'll realise you probably have different priorities and you don't need to have everything your friends do. If you can stand on your own two feet alongside them, then you can have that glorious female solidarity where you reap the mutual benefits of having someone in your life who shares many of your experiences and knows what that's like. What it is to be a female in the workplace, to be a female in the home, to be a mother, to be a sister. Having that kind of friendship and therefore all that advice you can call on, that person in your life who you can pick up the phone to and talk about anything with, knowing that you have got their support, empathy and help, is about one of the most important gifts you can have.

Success to me now is knowing that I am enough. Knowing that I already possess everything I need and all that makes me happy. Success is feeling rooted, appreciating what you have right now and being content. You will no doubt achieve so much in your life, but right now you are already enough. For me, this phrase has helped me more than 'learning to love myself', because we all have tough days and sometimes loving yourself feels like a stretch too far. I think the first step to that is knowing that you're enough.

It's wonderful to have dreams and to pursue them with positivity and excitement. But we also need to live in the moment. I have a tendency to overplan. I can rush forwards, and sometimes I'm very guilty of living in a future that I never quite get to because I'm always planning the next bit and the next bit. I know when I am doing this that what I really need to do is come back to myself and come back to the moment. If you are only focused on the future and always planning for tomorrow or the next day, or the next year, or when you've saved enough money for the house, or when you've passed that exam, or when you've met the one, then you will likely miss out on the richness of your present. You won't experience these things until you're there, and when you are there, you'll be planning and dreaming of other things.

Even when you are able to identify your true goals, the ones that come from your heart, it's still so important to focus on where you are right now because it is the only thing that is actually real. It's really important just to stop and think, where am I today? What am I doing with my day? What would I like today? What do I need today? Who can I love today? What can I celebrate today?

We can all dream big, and as long as we are not missing out on appreciating the present moment, then it can fun. The first step on the road to doing something is imagining yourself doing it, after all. But sometimes, if you set your goals too high or too huge, they can seem utterly overwhelming, and because you don't know how to get there it's tempting to give up. I find that breaking things down into more manageable pieces, creating mini goals, mini targets that you can tick off as you go along, helps reduce that feeling.

For example, I wanted to work on how I tend to rush from one thing to the next, my mind going at a hundred miles an hour, busy with all the things I have to do. I have tried so many things that can help me – both big and small – and one of the small goals I set was to make myself a cup of tea in the morning and drink it before it got cold, rather than forgetting about it while I tried to do seven other things at the same time! Not a big or immediately life-changing goal, but it helped me. Then I was introduced to drinking cacao – made from unroasted beans from the cacao tree, and an ancient medicine that has been used for millennia – and my simple tea-drinking goal transformed into a morning ritual that helps me switch off my busy brain for a couple of minutes and start the day in a way I feel good about.

Another simple goal I have identified recently is that I would like to read more. I know the reason why I don't do this as much as I'd like is that it's hard to find the time. After all, in our busy lives, so often a new goal requires a trade-off with time currently spent on something else. Belle is a brilliant reader, and so once or twice a week I am going to try to sit with her while she reads before bed and read my book too, until she gets tired and wants to turn out the light. I'm not going to do it every single night because I know that it's not realistic, as I will miss out on the time in the evening I like to spend with Dan. But this is another example of starting something quite simple, and then the likelihood is that it will grow quite naturally into a habit and something that's important to me, until I can't imagine not doing it.

First things first: when you set yourself a goal, who are you setting that goal for? Are you doing it for somebody else, or are you doing it for you? Are you doing it because it's what's expected of you, or are you doing it for you? Are you doing it because somebody else has told you to, or are you doing it for you? Ensuring the goal is something that's true to you should always be your starting point. Then, when you start to work towards that goal, how does it make you feel? Does it feel good? Does it feel like you should be doing this? Is this something that's making your heart sing? And if the answer's no, then maybe go back to the beginning and see who you're doing this for.

Almost all goals are achievable if they're what you really, really want to do, but if they're not, your mind often finds a way of sabotaging them. Apart from anything else, if they're not really what you want then it's so much harder to stay on the path towards something that deep, deep down was never right for you in the first place.

The moon provides me with a lot of inspiration for setting goals, and it reminds me to choose manageable goals or break them down into more bite-sized pieces so I don't become overwhelmed. Whenever there's a new moon, I sit myself down and I write all my intentions for that month, things that I'd like to achieve. Lots of them are just small, mini goals. For example: 'This month, I'm going to make sure I stretch more. I'm going to read a couple of pages of my book every night before I go to bed. I'm going to find a new podcast. I am going to take my children and our friend's dog and we're going to go for long walks and talk to each other.' This month, this is what I want to do, these are my goals. Sure, sometimes I have bigger, longer term things on my list, but I still tend to break them down into smaller elements, setting them as intentions at the beginning of the month. Then, over the course of the month, I work towards them, and when the full moon comes in the middle of the month it reminds me to take a moment to look over my list and see how I am getting on.

When the waning moon starts to disappear at the end of the month, I sit down and think, 'Right, what did I manage to tick off my list? What didn't I achieve this month, and why not? Was that a realistic goal? Was that something that I really, really wanted or was it something that I felt I should do?' And I know that with the new moon, I can start again; I can sort of correct it, recalibrate. I think having that monthly cycle, knowing that it doesn't matter if I don't achieve what I set out to achieve because I can start again, is a really good way of building those little mini successes throughout the year.

At the end of the year, you look back and you see, 'OK, here's the bigger picture.' All those little goals that have been achieved and ticked off were all part of this tapestry, all building to something greater. If you'd set all of these goals at the same time at the beginning of the year, it would have been overwhelming and you probably wouldn't have achieved that much. I really find that making things smaller and more manageable leads to greater success.

There's one more really important thing I want to say about success. Whatever you have decided that 'success' means to you, it is vital to know that in order to be successful, you have to fail so many times. There is so much good in failure because that's where you learn all of your lessons. It's great when things go well, of course, but that doesn't teach us as much. Not being afraid to fail is useful because it means that you'll give anything a go without holding back for fear of getting it wrong, of looking silly, of not

ROLE MODELS

As a young girl, my earliest role models came from Disney films. I still love the whole Disney experience – the magic and the fairy tales – but at the same time, I now recognise the problems with the messaging. If you are a beautiful princess then one day your prince will come and you'll get picked out and whisked away to live happily ever after. I can't think of one of those old-school Disney princesses that has a female friend. They are on their own. They might have a little animal that helps them out – but where is the female solidarity? Luckily, the new generation of Disney films, such as *Frozen*, seem to be redressing the balance, but so many of us grew up with problematic messaging. In the earlier films there is often a wicked stepmother or queen that wants the princess killed, so the only females around them are pitted against them. These are messages that slip through. If you're beautiful your prince will come, but you should be wary of other women.

Women being pitted against each other is nothing new, yet when women work together and support each other it is the most powerful and heady experience. One of the greatest examples I've ever seen of women coming together and sharing their absolute truth is the #MeToo movement, which has had a huge concurrent effect on so many other women and made such a difference; if you live your truth and come together with the women around you, and embrace being honest and supportive with one another, look at the shift that can happen.

My womenfolk are very, very important to me. My mother is a huge part of my life, and my sister and I are extremely close. We've lived together, we work together, we tell each other everything – there's nothing she doesn't know about my life, and vice versa.

I look up to the women in my life that are closest to me, particularly my mum and my sister, and those women, my womenfolk, who I have around me. They bring strength and foundation into my life. They hold me up, they listen to me, they create a space where I feel entirely comfortable to be me without any fear of being judged or not believed. We laugh together, we cry together. All of those big emotions are welcomed at any point, and it is this support network that enables me to function on a day-to-day basis.

I remember, when I was growing up, people would say that girls are so bitchy, that female friendships are toxic. Actually, I think this couldn't be more untrue. The connection I have with my girlfriends underpins my life. I hold them very close to me.

The women I work with are my heroes, too. In my job, I get to interview people who have been through the most extraordinary experiences and achieved so much. But I also admire the women working in TV behind the scenes, calling the shots (literally). They're forthright and fun. Live TV is an especially fast-paced working environment and you have to be assertive. What I see of many of these women at work is just the tip of the iceberg. Some have families, some run side-businesses or charities. Many of these women do all of this alongside raising families. Sometimes they have a strength of character that's silent, and sometimes it's upfront and out there. But always there's this underlying confidence that I love and admire.

Friends of mine have that quality within them too. They have a clear set of beliefs and a moral fibre, which draws me to them. They are all gorgeous and beautiful – of course! – but there's an attractiveness that shines through because of that quality of inner confidence. It's something I didn't always have myself, so I think that's probably why I am a little in awe of it.

We found it quite easy to name our boys. Particularly Harry, as that was Dan's grandfather's name. But when I found out that I was pregnant with a girl, for some reason it felt much more difficult to decide on a name. You don't want something that sounds too harsh, but nor do you want something too soft and fluffy. Like most of us, I thought about women I admired and looked around for things that had meaning for me.

I think I was eleven when *Beauty and the Beast* came out, and I loved it instantly. My mum took me to see it twice. To me, Belle was the rock-star Disney princess. Partly because she wasn't really a princess at all. She was an ordinary

The women I work with...inspire me to keep going

person who was practical and very brave; she loved books and she was the smartest person in her village. She was also the one who did the saving, rather than waiting around for a man to save her. So I wish I had a better story, but when I was trying to decide what to name my daughter, that's how 'Belle' made it onto the list!

When Emma Watson was cast in the live-action remake of *Beauty and the Beast*, she said in some interviews that she thought Belle was the most feminist of the Disney heroines, and that definitely chimed with how I felt as a kid, though I wouldn't have been able to articulate it as Emma did. So I was really surprised when she was berated by some for saying that, and her portrayal of Belle as an inventor was dismissed because in this new film she invents a washing machine. There was lots of analysis of the film story and questioning of its feminist credentials.

We have made so much progress by questioning things that had previously just been accepted, and I know we will continue to move things forward in this way. However, I do think that you can watch something or read something and analyse it and pull it apart to the point where you take all of the joy from it. Nothing is ever without fault – it would be dull and boring if it was.

Since I started writing this book and thinking about what beauty means, I began to consider my daughter Belle's name again, and what it means that I gave her this name, 'beauty'. In one sense, it could be a huge thing to live up to. But do you know what? I loved the name when I first knew I was having her and I love it even more now. On every level, she embodies what beauty *really* means. She is free-spirited and independent; someone who is already making her own rule book for life. She is confident in her own being, and so empathetic and kind. It's funny that I named her 'Beauty' when she was in my tummy as I think she is absolutely beautiful in every way, and with every day that passes, she lives up to her name more and more. I am so glad we called her Belle.

As a parent, I try to treat Belle in exactly the same way as I do my two sons. With the exception that every night I say to her, 'Night beautiful, night princess, night gorgeous!' I don't think it's wrong because she is such a beautiful soul, but I'm conscious that this isn't language I'd use around my sons so it's something I do need to think about.

I can't help but hope the feminist movement will become non-existent from my kids' point of view, in the sense that they will grow up with everyone totally equal and it will seem strange to them that equal rights and treatment was ever something that women had to fight for. And that me worrying about whether I should be calling Belle a beautiful princess will seem funny and so inconsequential to her.

I sometimes find the idea of being a role model myself very daunting, and I definitely suffer from mum guilt. But at the same time, I'm proud to be a working mum and I hope that it's good for all my children to see that, as a female in the workplace, I am right up there alongside any man in my industry. Their mummy and daddy are on equal ground; we both pay the bills and we both have a strong work ethic. And, actually, financially what we bring is irrelevant, as two humans we are equal. What they see around them at this stage is really important, I think, and I hope that by Dan and I simply living these roles that that will sink in and inform their own relationships as they grow. That's not to say I think all parents should work – this is my situation and my family and I can only talk about what's true to me and best for us.

I'm also conscious of role-modelling respectful relationships for them, as I know that what they see in us they will take forward into their own relationships – so what conversations are they hearing between their mum and dad? Dan and I always try to make sure we're completely aligned on anything to do with parenting, and that whenever we're talking to one another it is always with total respect and open communication. In our family, everybody has a voice that can be heard. The kids know that communication and listening to understand is a really important one for us. They know that it's good to discuss and explain, and that you must always talk about your feelings, if something's on your mind. We all hold that space in our family for one another to be able to talk about those things. But there is also a time to be quiet and to listen and to hear what someone else has got to say.

Over the years, I have begun to understand and become more comfortable with the fact that, as a woman, I'm a combination of lots of things. Yes, I've got this feminine, emotional softness, and I sometimes just want to be at home and to shut the door on the world, bake bread and do all those domestic things, but I also have a business side. I love my job and I love having a career and thinking about where it can go. I don't know what I'd do if I couldn't go to work.

I'm not failing feminism if I get joy from my home and from being with my children. I am not failing my family because I go out to work for the rewards I get from it, rather than necessity. It's about being able to have those different sides and knowing one does not negate the other; they can exist and work together in balance. That's because as people we are more complex than simply the labels of businesswoman or homemaker. You can be both.

That's not 'trying to have it all' – I'm just trying to do what feels right for me. What I like and what I'm interested in. All those different things that make me 'me' should be able to sing in harmony. One voice doesn't have to be louder; they can all sing together.

BEAUTY & SEXUALITY

Who decides what's beautiful? Looking back in time, it is generally men who have created the parameters for what we perceive as physically beautiful in a woman. But when I think about even the most famous traditional beauties, I'm drawn to something other than their looks...

Marilyn Monroe and Audrey Hepburn must be the two most iconic beauties of the twentieth century. One a vivacious and curvy blonde; the other a willowy and elegant brunette. Their images and the ideals of femininity they represent had such a big impact, and their legacies still influence trends and what we see as beautiful today. And I love them too. Looking at my bookshelves I can count ten books on Marilyn Monroe and six on Audrey Hepburn.

I was first drawn to Marilyn Monroe because of that iconic image of her: the red lip and black flicked eyeliner. That stunning drop-dead gorgeous blonde look. It's a look that stops you in your tracks. As the years have gone on, though, I've fallen in love with her more because of her vulnerability. The pictures that I love of her aren't those when she's done up as a siren, strapped into a tight wiggle dress, or white skirt blowing up around her ears. They're stunning images but they remind me of the male gaze, the male perception of beauty. The images I love are the shots of her on a beach with a blanket, hardly any make-up on, hair absolutely not done, looking incredibly natural. You see the real person – not the manufactured blonde bombshell; the image that everyone projected their lustful thoughts onto and made the standard for what a sexy, attractive woman should aspire to be. She was never taken seriously and was prevented from being her true self; she was taken advantage of physically, emotionally and professionally.

I read that when Marilyn died, her body was interred in a crypt in what was then a quiet, out-of-the-way Hollywood cemetery. When the man who owned the crypt in the wall above hers died he asked to be turned face down in his coffin so that he'd be lying on top of her. It is one of the most disgusting things I've ever read in my life. Then, Hugh Hefner bought the plot next to her, explaining, 'Spending eternity next to Marilyn is too sweet to pass up,' and was interred there following his death in 2017. After she became a star, and without her consent, Hefner had published nude photos of Marilyn, which she'd been paid $50 for back when she was a struggling actress in need of money. She was desperately embarrassed and Hefner made a fortune, launching *Playboy* and kick-starting his empire off the back of them. Hefner exploited her both before and after her death and my heart breaks for her.

The other classic icon is Audrey Hepburn: the little black dress, the chicness, her innocence and, yet again, vulnerability. She was glamorous without being dangerous. Audrey's son has said his mother didn't think she was beautiful, that she had self-esteem issues. Knowing that even this universally regarded beauty had the same anxieties about her looks that so many of us do only makes her more appealing to me.

I was initially fascinated by these women because their beauty provides escapism. It's almost like looking at a sunset; their beauty appears so unreal and unobtainable that you can only daydream about it, looking up to them like goddesses. But that's the way their images were sold to us by Hollywood studio execs. Anything that humanised these women, or challenged our views of them as perfect, was discarded. We weren't ready to hear what they had to say, we couldn't accept that external perfection could be coupled with internal struggle. I fell into the trap of thinking my iconic women were flawless. But when I bought those books and dived into both Monroe and Hepburn's lives, I learned that it was all there – the struggle and the vulnerability – hidden in plain sight, until, as in the case of Marilyn, it became public in the most tragic of circumstances. I identify far more with this side of these two goddesses and am grateful that our modern icons can be fully rounded humans, beautifully flawed.

These days, the women I really admire tend to be older women. That might be because now I have reached my forties, my perspective has naturally shifted and I look up to women who are blazing a trail ahead of me. But there's something far deeper and more profound about the beauty of a woman who has lived a life, and all that she is and all that she has learned shines through in everything she does, from what she chooses to wear to how she holds herself and the confidence she exudes.

I find myself being drawn to women not because of how they look physically, but because of their strength. I think there's a bit inside of me that goes: 'Wow, look at you, you're doing this. You can stand on your own two feet and be heard.' That, to me, is mesmerisingly attractive; it grabs me more than anything, and it's how I want to be.

So much has changed in the world since Marilyn Monroe was making her most famous films and being both celebrated and punished for being this sexy and outwardly beautiful woman. But in other ways we still have a long way to go. Women can be sensual and sexual beings, and we should be able to enjoy that. But definitely in my life, and I think it's the same for a lot of women, this has sometimes been hijacked by others, who take ownership of it until you feel like it doesn't belong to you anymore. Then you become disconnected from your own sensuality and sexuality because it feels risky, and hiding from it is just a safer space to be in.

Our behaviour is shaped by our experience. If people behave badly towards us then we begin to wonder whether it's something we're doing, or the way we look – that maybe we're *inviting* it in. Even now, there is still a lurking attitude of, 'If you dress like that you're asking for it,' or

'Well, you shouldn't wear such a short skirt,' or, 'If you dance like that, who are you dancing for?' We're not allowed to own our sexuality for fear of attracting unwanted attention, even aggression, and this is just nonsense. It's so unfair. We should be allowed to express every part of ourselves, including our sexuality, without fear. This is another way that outside influences can make us lose sense of who we really are, what we want, how we feel.

But we don't have to stand for it. In 2018, as part of the Time's Up movement, stars at the Grammy Awards in New York wore white roses on the red carpet to show their support for ending sexual harassment in their industry. Then, a month later, in February, it was decided that we'd do the same thing in the UK at the Brit Awards.

I love the Brit Awards. It's one of my favourite nights of the year – it's rock and roll and always a great party atmosphere. I can get dressed up, have a fun night with lots of people I know, and listen to some incredible music. When I go to TV awards, that's fun too, but it's more like work: the press want to know about TV shows you're doing, and sometimes I'll be presenting an award. But music is a different world that I'm not a part of, so the BRITs feels like a night off where I can let my hair down.

In 2018, I gave a lot of thought to what I could wear and how I could do my make-up that felt right in the context of my thoughts and feelings around supporting this really important Time's Up movement. I chose a beautiful white dress with feathers around the hem to match the white rose I'd be carrying. It was bold and fun to wear – almost like a tuxedo jacket with black buttons, ending in this soft, feminine fluffy bit around the edge.

It was a great night, but then when we went to leave, there were all these paparazzi with their lenses low to the floor, desperately trying to catch a glimpse of our knickers as we got into taxis. I couldn't believe it. I'd walked up the red carpet a few hours earlier, holding that rose with pride for the Time's Up movement, a campaign to end sexual harassment, and then there were these male photographers trying to take a photo up my skirt.

I rarely get involved publicly in anything contentious or political, but I felt compelled that night to make it known that this behaviour wasn't OK, so I posted about it on social media. The contrast between all these incredible women walking down the red carpet holding those roses, full of hope, and what we faced at the end of the night was so stark. The post had a huge reaction and it resonated with a lot of people.

One woman, Gina Martin, got in touch and she ended up coming on to *This Morning*. She'd had her own experience of upskirting when she was at a gig and a man put his phone between her legs and took a picture. She reported it to the police, who said they couldn't do anything because it wasn't a crime in England (though in Scotland upskirting has been illegal since 2010). So she had started a campaign against the practice and had taken it to Parliament. A year later, she did it: in 2019, the Voyeurism (Offences) Bill was passed by Parliament, making upskirting a criminal offence. I think that's really inspiring and just goes to show that we don't have to accept the way things are.

This is an example of how a campaign can bring about an important legal change. However, there are times when it's not so simple. Now I am older, I better understand that while I cannot control the behaviour of other people, I can control the impact that it has on me, on how I think about myself and how I go forward with my life. I can control my connection with my own sensuality and sexuality. It belongs to me. It's mine.

I now recognise that at times in my life when the volume of that has been turned down low, where I just couldn't hear it, I lost touch with myself. If this resonates with you, then please know it doesn't have to stay like that and it does get better. It does take time and it does take work, but a big step towards changing things is to give yourself the space and the permission to listen, to tune into your body and your sensuality, to claim it back.

Beauty is a big puzzle of tiny little pieces pulled from all aspects of your life, and actually so few of the pieces come simply from what's on the outside. Who do I want to look nice for? Who do I do it for? Me, always. Women shouldn't feel guilty for wanting to be sexy and sensual. We should feel comfortable with these aspects of ourselves because they are ours. Our sexuality, our sensuality, it belongs to *us*. And it is wonderful to share it on our terms. To have fun sharing it, and to enjoy sharing it as much as we want to. But always on our terms.

icons

Glinda the Good Witch from *The Wizard of Oz* was one of my earliest beauty icons. The moment in the film where it goes from black and white to technicolour is still magical, even all these years later. Dorothy opens the door into Oz and the highly saturated colours are almost overwhelming, like a beautiful tsunami sweeping over your senses. Glinda appears out of a bubble, wearing an enormous pink frock – exactly what every child would imagine a glamorous fairy to wear. I loved that dress, and I would still wear it now on *Dancing on Ice*, given half a chance!

When I grew up a bit, like most young girls in the 1990s, I was influenced by the style of the girl bands of the era. All Saints in their Timberlands, cargo pants and asymmetric vest tops, and the **Spice Girls** with their big shoes and big attitudes, were a million miles away from fairy dresses, but I recognised it as something fun and empowering. Especially the way the Spice Girls wore outfits that reflected their personalities. Looking back, I think it probably introduced a generation of young girls to the idea that you dressed for you, to reflect who you are and how you feel. There was a sense of freedom in what they wore and how they approached fashion and beauty, and, importantly, it felt like they were doing it for themselves – not for men, or to conform to what was traditionally seen as attractive.

Then there's **Debbie Harry**. Her glamorous and gritty punk style has had such a major influence on fashion. With her strong eye make-up and vintage T-shirts she is the godmother of that classic rock chick look. As the lead singer of Blondie, she is the ultimate frontwoman, and every photo of her oozes an effortlessness and a fearlessness that you just can't look away from.

1

2

I have a photograph of her in my bedroom because I just think she is gorgeous and want to look at her every day. She inspires me.

While we are talking about a kind of fearless glamour, I've always been fascinated by **Joan Collins**. When I was young, I used to get into my mum's bed and we'd watch *Dynasty* together. Joan played Alexis Carrington, this wickedly cold woman who was always immaculately turned out, with these incredible 1980s dresses and shoulder pads – I was mesmerised by her. Joan was born in Paddington, West London, and began appearing in Hollywood films in the 1950s, so in a way she's Britain's connection to that era of Hollywood glamour. I've been lucky enough to meet her a few times and she's as fabulous in real life as you'd expect. She knows exactly what works for her and what doesn't – I think she's probably an expert at applying make-up. She once told me that Marilyn Monroe used to do her eye flick with a Lancôme eyeliner and I felt like I'd been given some deep secret that nobody else knew!

And then there are women who have broken the glass ceiling when it came to what historically has been considered as beautiful. **Josephine Baker**, the first black woman to star in a major motion picture, was a phenomenon. As well as being a dancer, singer and mother, she used her platform for change. She was born in the United States and when she witnessed the St Louis race riots, she knew acceptance and opportunity were not going to come for her in the US at that time. She travelled to Paris to pursue her passion for performing and here she was celebrated for her talent. She was one of the most photographed women of the time, famed for turning down 1,000 marriage proposals. Picasso and Hemingway adored her, referring to her as a 'black Venus.' She has been accused of perpetuating racial stereotypes with some of her choices of costume and style of dance, while others see her as a victim of fetishisation. Josephine empowered herself.

3

4

She did what she had to do to get what she wanted from life. There can be no blame laid at her feet, in my opinion. She changed the way black women were perceived and was buried with military honours in Paris. Princess Grace Kelly, another iconic beauty, was in the church to pay her respects. We owe this iconic beauty a huge amount; she truly was a trailblazer.

Whenever I go on holiday I always wish I could look like **Penelope Cruz** in *Vicky Cristina Barcelona*. She looks fantastic, with her big smoky eyes and bohemian style, and hair a bit like a messier Brigitte Bardot! Penelope Cruz has an iconic beauty,

5

6

7

but it's sort of given a wildness in this role – she plays the character of María Elena with this untamed passion, an out-of-control intensity that draws you in.

Dolly Parton is just a dreamboat. I love her music and I love her look – her hair, her make-up, her outfits, her costumes. She's an incredibly talented songwriter and musician. She's carved her own path through the difficult world of music and showbiz for decades with such grace and self-assurance. I think her look is the armour that she's worn to protect herself. When you watch clips of her on TV as a young woman, you see this super-smart, bright talent. She constructed an identity with the big hair, the eyelashes, the layers of make-up, the amazing costumes, and she owned it all. Her 'Dollyisms', her quick reactions and smart quips to anybody who dares question the way she looks, just strengthen the message that she's trying to put out there. Dolly's magic shows us that we don't have to stop wearing sequins and grow old decorously;

we can do whatever we want.

Take **Charlotte Rampling**, for example. She was an icon of the 1960s, known for making arthouse films, and she's had a long and fascinating career following her own path. She's magnetic, I think in part because there is a mystery to her. She has these eyes that can almost see through you. At every stage of her life and career she has always seemed to be in complete command of her sensuality and sexuality. When she's spoken about ageing in the past, she describes it as something that she chooses not to have a relationship with, asking, 'Isn't it just another way of having passion for life?'

What we can learn from Charlotte is to choose where we put our energies. If we waste them worrying about our image, ageing, what we're losing, what's leaving our lives, then how can we expect to sit in passion and joy and wonder? Charlotte, I want to be you when I grow up.

If **Dame Helen Mirren** sees herself as having a relationship with ageing then it seems to be a wholly positive one. She's always been beautiful and sexy, but there just seems to be something so unique about her as she has got older. It really, really suits her. She has the most incredible hair and it's always beautifully cut but she's not afraid to play with the colour. I remember when she dyed it a soft, bubblegum pink, breaking all the rules of what older women are supposed to do, and it looked fabulous. She has a marvellous twinkle in her eye and always seems to be having fun – in life and with what she wears. She occasionally walks the red carpet with a pair of Perspex platform shoes, or 'stripper shoes' as she calls them, poking out from underneath a ballgown, like a witty and sexy wink.

Perhaps **Michaela Coel** is the beauty icon we have the most to learn from. I feel like we are watching her evolve in real time. She draws viewers in with her incredibly generous writing and takes us along for her ride in such a raw, passionate and honest way. Not only is she a stand-out beauty but, more importantly, she is living in her beauty with true authenticity. She has said before that not caring what other people think is the most important part of self-care. For me, this is Michaela's true inspirational draw. I believe you only get to this level of freedom and clarity after some very hard-fought and won battles.

BODIES

When I was at school, at age fifteen, we had to do some work experience. I'd already been approached to do some modelling work and thought it might be helpful to learn more about how the industry works so I wrote to loads of different fashion and modelling agencies trying to get a placement. Models 1 wrote back and said that I could do my work experience there. I was so excited – I thought I was going to go on all these fashion shoots…! In reality, every day for a week I got the train from my local station, Hassocks in Sussex, to the London office of the agency, where I mostly made lots of tea. But I still loved it. My other job was to return the models' portfolios, which had been sent back from various places, to the 'library'. I had to go through them and, using cleaning fluid – I think it was lighter fluid, weirdly – on a cloth, wipe any fingerprints off the pages. This wasn't really necessary, they were just trying to keep me busy, but it gave me the opportunity to see all these women's faces staring back at me. All these incredibly strong women looking amazing and beautiful. And every so often, one of these tall, striking women would walk into the agency and sit down to have a chat, and I thought, *wow*. I was in awe of their beauty.

I have never looked like the women I'd seen striding across the office during my work experience, but I did work in modelling for a bit. It wasn't long after my work experience that I went to The Clothes Show and was spotted there. I learned then that there are two sides of modelling: the tall goddesses who do catwalk modelling, and the commercial girls, who have the big smiles and do the cornflake ads – or the sanitary towel ads, in my case. Both make great money, but one is slightly more glamorous than the other. I also found out then that I'm not one of the goddess women, but I am one of the commercial girls, and I've got a cheeky smile.

I was given an A-to-Z of London (you had to have a paper map in those days, of course!) and sent to casting calls all over the city with a bunch of other girls who had just been signed up too. I loved walking around London with these girls. We were called 'new faces' because we were so young – I was still about fifteen, I think. It was an amazing learning curve for me because I threw myself in at the deep end and had to suddenly find all this confidence from nowhere. It wasn't something that came naturally to me. So I was forcing myself into uncomfortable situations. When I'd try out for a commercial, they'd give me a script and I'd just have to go in and do it, on camera, in front of ten people, all watching me. And if it didn't go well it would feel so embarrassing.

Soon, however, I realised my body was developing in a way that didn't fit the modelling bill anymore. I had decided to do some travelling, and while I was in Sydney I went to an agency to meet the booker. I'd hoped I could do some modelling there and maybe live in Sydney for a bit. The booker was really nice. Afterwards, I spoke to my London agency to see what she'd said, and the comment I got back was: 'We'll put her weight down to healthy eating while travelling.'

I just thought, wow. I could look in the mirror and see that I was seventeen and tiny. I'd travelled the world at that point and was having a great time. I was seeing real life and experiencing lots of exciting things for the first time. So to hear a comment like that was a complete and utter shock. I saw for myself the brutal and, in my opinion, ugly side of what I'd always thought was the most beautiful place, and I realised then that it was not for me.

I knew that if I was going to compete with these other girls, I was going to have to drastically change my diet and how I lived. I don't know where my resolve came from, but I just decided it wasn't for me. Sometimes I look back at my youth and I admire the person I was then because I think I listened to my gut a lot more than I have in my later life. Something told me that trying to force my body to be a certain shape wasn't on, that it was not a good way to live.

I think now that was a really brave decision to make because the modelling industry – being part of it, being hailed as one of those beautiful people – is so alluring. Especially when you're seventeen and you've just come out of that awkward adolescent stage and all you want is for people to think that you are growing up to be a beautiful woman. Or at least, I thought that was what was important to me at the time. But still, it was not enough, not so important that I was willing to damage myself in some way. I so admire that seventeen-year-old and the strength I had then; somehow I had a voice that was so strong that it wasn't going to be drowned out by any external influences.

I've interviewed plenty of people whose decisions when they were teenagers still affect them today. It's so difficult when you are young and you're faced with a job or a situation that's is very glamorous that you'd do anything to be a part of it – even to your own detriment. I'm proud I didn't fall foul of that, but I also know that I was very lucky. I absolutely owe it to the fact that I had a really strong, nurturing foundation in my family. I knew I was loved and supported completely, and I can only thank my mum and dad for helping to give me a strong enough sense of self to know that putting myself in any kind of danger wasn't worth it.

I came back to London, and on one of my first days of modelling back in the city, I was about to head home when one of my girlfriends asked me to go to a casting with her. It wasn't on my list but she didn't want to go on her own. We girls stuck together then, so I went with her and blagged my way into this casting and it turned out to be for a TV show. And I got it. It was an ITV show called *S Club TV*. I was an utterly rubbish presenter then, but that was the beginning of the next chapter for me. It was a real sliding doors moment – had I not listened to what was right and true for myself back in Sydney, life could have gone in a completely different direction. It was an important early lesson to not be someone else, that good things happen when you listen to your inner voice, the one that makes you 'you'. First you have to listen to what

good things happen when you listen to your inner voice

your inner voice is saying, then you have to follow through with your actions. Sometimes the second bit is the hardest.

Even now, as a grown woman who has done a lot to try to reconnect with her true inner thoughts and feelings, as the mother of three children, I look back in awe at that seventeen-year-old who refused to damage herself in any way because some people more powerful than her had implied that there was something 'wrong' with her. There have certainly been times when I have wondered where that strength has gone.

I think we all feel like that sometimes as we get older. On the one hand, youth can be a time of such insecurity, of not knowing who we are yet. But on the other hand, it's a time of great freedom, when we don't have years of experience and information overcomplicating our feelings. You are green but your eyes are wide open to new experiences. That black and white certainty, that immediate sense of what is right and wrong, can seem a bit naive and simplistic when you look back on it from a place where you have learned, from experience, that there are actually many shades of grey – but it made decision-making easier. I was much more likely to just go with my gut. I wonder if you can know too much when you are older.

I don't know which is the better way to live. The experience you have and the wealth of information you take in is a glorious part of getting older, but it's no good having access to all this knowledge and understanding of the world if it means you don't have clarity of instinct. It's not easy, to say the least. But the ideal would be to find a way to access that clarity of youth while still basing your decisions on a richer pool of information.

Of course, people did not stop having opinions of how I looked when I stopped modelling. I have had my body scrutinised my entire life, and I came to the conclusion, actually quite a long time ago, that I just wouldn't be part of the story. But even so, we've all got insecurities and hang-ups. We let them influence how we speak to ourselves, and sometimes they even stop us doing something we would otherwise like to do. How many times have you missed out on things because of poor body image? Have you ever passed up on a night out because you didn't like what you were wearing? Have you ever not been in the sea on holiday because you didn't want to put on swimwear or take the towel from around your waist? How many times have you been so self-conscious about how you look and what you're wearing that it's stopped you having fun with your friends, playing with your kids or just being really in the moment?

The recent body positivity movement has been amazing in the way it has championed bodies of all shapes and sizes and encouraged us to reject this idea of perfection that society has created, and celebrate the skin we're in. But I know some women feel it's too much of a stretch for them, just yet, to be happy with every single bit of their body. And that's OK. In some ways, your insecurities are what make you 'you'. So listen to them, stop hiding them. It's when we push them down inside us as if they are something shameful that it becomes damaging. What is it that you're insecure about? And do you know why? Are you insecure about something that somebody else has made the rules on? Are they your rules? What do *you* feel about it? Work out where it's coming from, because I'm sure that most of the time it's not really coming from you.

We always look at what we don't have, and we often focus on ways that we could look better on the outside. But it's important to look the other way and say, do you know what? I'm in good health. My legs work, my digestive system functions, I'm healthy. Sometimes it's good to remind yourself to appreciate what you have. I know it's not easy because we are bombarded with images of perfection all the time, and they're always there lurking in the corners of our mind. It's hard not to compare ourselves to others. But looking good on the outside doesn't help us if we don't feel good on the inside; if we don't stop to appreciate all the things we have. I think we all know that, really. If you start a day with negative thoughts about yourself they will hang around you all day and you'll walk through life with them. But I want to give you a gentle reminder that there is another option. There is another way.

How do you talk to yourself when it comes to your body? For example, I could look in the mirror and say to myself, 'If only my bum was smaller so I could wear skinny jeans. I'm getting older now and I have to wear bikinis that have got a little bit of a supporting structure. But I would love to wear a tiny little bikini and run around on the beach like I used to do! That's just not going to happen. Oh my god, I'm getting older.'

However, I could change that conversation to sound like this: 'This is a body that had three happy children and it knew exactly what to do; it just knew how to keep those children safe inside me. I was able to give birth to life. My breasts were able to feed my children, they knew what to do. My body is healthy and strong. So many people have underlying health conditions, but my body has maintained me and kept me fit and healthy and able to go into work. When I've been stressed, I've been able to go for a run, and when I've been too much in my head, I can do Pilates or stretch and get out of my head and back in my body.'

Once I reframe that I start to think, 'Yeah, that's amazing. That's pretty cool, actually.' And you start to change the way you feel about yourself. Same body, same person, different conversation.

So listen to the conversations you're having with yourself. Would you be OK with someone speaking to your partner, or your child, or your mother, or your friend in that way? If not, then it might be time to find a way to be kinder to yourself, to change the conversation. If that voice is with you all the time, wanting more from you, putting you down, imagine the damage that causes.

It seems everybody has got an opinion on diet and exercise. I don't want to add fuel to the flames. We all know that getting out and going for a walk is good for us – not just physically but mentally too. We know that we should be drinking lots of water, eating fruit and veg. Nourish your body; look after that machine that is so precious and unique to you. Feed it a variety of healthy, nutritious foods. But indulge yourself too. Celebrate food. There are so many joyous moments that happen around food. The connection we feel when we eat together around a table or we make a meal for people we love; the conversation, the laughs, the memories that are made when we sit down together and share food – this is what eating is about, not about cutting out foods or trying to make our bodies smaller. Look after this body. You only have one. Make it strong, without being a slave to it. Keep it active, without punishing yourself.

As a person who lives in her head and has lots of thoughts rushing around all the time, bringing my awareness into my body really does help. That doesn't mean I'm going to be hammering the treadmill for hours and hours – even just stretching my muscles brings me back into my body and helps me connect with myself. I find that movement, whether it's a good walk or dancing with my girlfriends, is incredibly grounding and freeing. I can't think of many things that are more fun than throwing myself around my friend's kitchen with a glass of wine in my hand, dancing to the radio and not even caring if anybody's looking at me, because if they are, I know that I'm fully supported and loved by the woman standing next to me, doing exactly the same thing. Don't worry about the latest workout trend – just move. Move and feel free and get into your body and feel your body. Give your head a break.

If you know it would be good for your mental and physical health to get moving more, rather than saying, 'I'm on a diet and a fitness plan,' say, 'I'm looking after my body. I'm going to nourish my body. I'm going to get into my body.' Then you're not stuck in some sort of regime that feels a lot like a punishment that you in no way deserve. You're beginning a new ritual that's for you. It sounds simple but it's funny how just changing the way you think about these things and speak to yourself can make a big difference.

Let's change the way we think about our bodies and how we treat them. You can either look at your body as an object to be desired and whittled down to minimal proportions, only ever at its ultimate when on the beach in a bikini, with no muffin top, tanned and smooth as a balloon. Or – and I would suggest this one – you see your body as an incredible machine that couldn't be created by the best scientists in the world. It is a living, breathing miracle. It can be the gateway to life. It can allow you to get from A to B. It can touch, hold, hug. It has an onboard computer that not only thinks and reasons, but makes connections and loves. It's such a wondrous thing, and regardless of what shape or size it comes in, it's a miracle. You have been blessed by the fact that you have a body, and if you are lucky enough to have a healthy body, then even more so. It is yours and it is unique to you.

'You are a living, breathing miracle'

FEELING
BEAUTIFUL FIRST

What was your first experience of feeling beautiful? It is important to me to consider how my ideas have been shaped, so I've been trying to think of a time growing up when I first became aware of what beauty was, what it represented.

Beauty and cosmetics weren't really a big deal for me when I was younger; they weren't things I was particularly interested in. But getting dressed up for special occasions was something to be cherished and celebrated. My first memory of wanting to look my best was as a little girl, maybe three years old, in the lead-up to Christmas. We'd always go to the panto and have a Christmas meal with our grandparents, and I loved the sense of occasion, getting dressed up and feeling, I guess, beautiful. I had one outfit I'd wear for all of those special days. One year, I remember going to a shop with my mum and trying on lots of beautiful dresses. They had a hoop in the bottom with layers of petticoats, and a couple had a bell sewn into them so when you walked you tinkled and sounded like Tinkerbell.

But if we're considering our first experience of feeling beautiful, it also makes sense to ask: when was your first experience of *not* feeling beautiful? Were you told by that kid in class, 'You're ugly!' Was that safe ground that your parents built for you – always calling you 'beautiful' and 'princess' – destroyed in one fell swoop when you were called something horrible by somebody in the playground? And, of course, choosing to believe that bully is easier than believing your parents because it feeds the insecurity already inside you.

Adolescence can be even crueller than the bullies because your body changes shape, and as it prepares for adulthood, puberty kicks in. Your skin changes, you get acne, you don't quite know if you're a child or an adult, and your brain is doing crazy things. Suddenly you're looking in the mirror and you're not recognising the person that you are. You're adapting and changing and your hormones are raging. How did you feel about yourself then? I think nearly all teenagers would say that when they look in the mirror they don't like what they see.

Adolescence is the doorway to the next stage of life. It's when your body and your personality is making itself anew, preparing for the person you are going to be. In a sense, each spot is a badge of honour, a sign that your body is preparing for growth, for your next adventure. But we certainly don't see it like that when it's happening to us, and we feel confused and insecure.

Teenagers today gorge on social media. Now you can put filter after filter over your entire body and face, you can shrink or enlarge any part of yourself. You can make yourself into something else online. We often measure ourselves against what society and the media deem right and perfect, which so often means that suddenly you're living someone else's truth and not your own. And now we're self-edited on social media, too. We can make our

Why do we aspire to be more beautiful? Are we doing it for ourselves?

noses smaller, our cheekbones higher, our lips plumper – then if we choose to we can go and get it all injected and changed in real life so that we look how the filters created in Silicon Valley make us look on our phone screens. And when hormones are raging, and there is this constant stream of filtered and distorted images to contend with, how do you cope with that? How can you ever feel beautiful? How can you ever feel comfortable in your own skin, when you are trying to achieve something that is utterly impossible? It's hard enough as an adult who grew up before all of this existed.

Why do we aspire to be more beautiful? Are we doing it for ourselves? I guess that's the right question. Are we doing it to change how we appear to other people? Whether that be friends, or on social media to gain followers, to gain fans. To appeal to men? Because we think it will make others love us more?

It's not a bad thing to want to be beautiful; it doesn't make you a bad person to want to make the best of yourself on the outside. But it needs to be part of a richer tapestry of life, with all these different threads coming from different places. It needs to be a beauty that is true to you, not a beauty that has been pushed onto you because it's the look of the moment on Instagram. It has to be your beauty, your truth. This constant noise of collective opinions from external influences surrounds us, when really we need to judge beautiful from within, from our hearts, from who we are inside. Get out of your head and into your heart.

Consider the amount of time you have spent thinking about how much smaller your bum could be, how much smaller your nose could be, how much whiter your teeth could be, how you wish you had fewer wrinkles – all these trivial things. How much mental space do you waste on those things? What else could you be doing with that time? Where else could that focus and attention go? How freeing would it be to wake up in the morning and look in the mirror and say, 'Morning! How are you today? What do you need today?', rather than, 'Oh God, you again. You look so old, so tired. My gosh, you've got a spot. Oh, where are your cheekbones?'

I don't want my daughter feeling that she needs to look a certain way to be considered beautiful by other people. That she has to cover her freckles with an inch of foundation. I don't want her feeling that her nose is too big or her lips aren't big enough. The rulebook of what beauty is needs to be torn up and thrown out the window. And it's up to us to be part of that.

The way we feel about ourselves and how we see beauty is a journey with different stages that eventually combine together. Sometimes we need to unpack these individual components and question them, to strip back all of those ideals that we have accepted as 'normal' or 'perfect'. Society has told us that beauty looks a certain way. And it's normally youth. And yes, youth is beautiful, of course; there is an innocent beauty in youth. However, there is beauty in every step of life, and it's about changing the perception that the only way to be beautiful is to be young, to have a flat stomach and a pert bum. That is not the only way to be beautiful. It's a specific set of a beliefs that we've just decided is the only way. Or rather, it has been decided for us. There is a real freedom when you let go of that. Beauty doesn't have to be put into a certain box. Beauty comes in all shapes, sizes, colours, ages.

Being able to accept yourself as you truly are is beauty. Believing and understanding that what makes you different is what makes you beautiful. True belief in that is an unbeatable thing. An unbeatable power. Beauty is loving the difference in yourself, which enables you to love the difference in other people. After all, how can you love difference in other people if you don't love it in yourself?

We need to create a space for everyone to stop looking at what's on the outside and start looking at what's on the inside. Love that, feel that, vibe off that. Think about what feels good. What's going to highlight who you are. Not what's going to get the most likes on social media, or what you think other people will approve of. It's so important to put these foundations in place because then you can have fun with all the other stuff from a place of real solid ground. Then you can play with the outside, and arrange your wardrobe and experiment with the make-up bag. And, actually, that's what we're going to do next in the next part of the book.

I've written a lot about self-care in these pages; it is a really important part of this book. Taking time for yourself and coming up with those little rituals of peace and quiet are soothing and connect you to who you are. Thinking, how am I today? Who am I today? How am I feeling today? But self-care is also related to beauty and make-up, because if we want them to be, they can be part of our rituals too. Just because I'm looking inward, that doesn't mean I can't look outward, too...

MEMORIES OF
MAKE-UP MAGIC

As a child, what images of beauty were around you? What did you perceive beauty to be? Have you ever thought about how you were introduced to the idea as a child? I have happy memories of going to the make-up hall at Selfridges with my mum. Getting the train into London felt like a big adventure anyway, but when we walked into the amazing old department store, past the dazzling array of lipsticks, powders and all sorts of unknown products in glass bottles, I felt so glamorous. My mum would stride across the shiny floor between the tall white columns to reach the Estée Lauder counter because that was her favourite. She wore this one pink lipstick and she would wait until Selfridges had a special offer on. She'd buy a mascara and lipstick and get a bag with another lipstick and a nail varnish – though often in a colour she'd never wear.

My mother is very beautiful, and at school I'd feel proud when she came to events because she didn't look like the other mums. To me, she was glamorous; she always had a dress on, she always wore lipstick. And having a parent that liked to dress up meant I absorbed by osmosis the idea of dressing up and beauty being synonymous in some way.

At the same time, though, my mum is a hands-on, practical person and she's never been afraid to roll her sleeves up. When I was young, I would come down in the morning and she might have been gardening for two hours, raking the leaves or moving logs from one pile to another, or she'd have stripped the downstairs bathroom of wallpaper ready to do some painting. Mum was cook, cleaner, mother, wife – everything. She ran the house and didn't worry about how she looked when she was at home, looking after us. She has always been very comfortable in her own skin.

However, when she went out, she liked to make the best of herself, to look nice, which she always did. Still, I remember that she would then take her make-up off with soap and water – not many of us would do that nowadays! She didn't have lotions and potions everywhere; the contents of her dressing table were pretty simple. I didn't get make-up know-how from my mum – her main piece of advice was to put your lipstick on or everyone will think you're exhausted. And she still says that to me now, as if a jot of lipstick is going to wave a magic wand and make me look like I've had a twelve-hour sleep!

I started learning about make-up as a teenager by doing makeovers with my friends. They'd come over and we'd take turns to sit at the little desk in my bedroom. I'd get all my mum's make-up and we'd look in the mirror and change our hair and try out different looks – we didn't know what we were doing but we had a great time doing it. We'd seen the before-and-after style makeovers in *Just Seventeen*, and that gave us the idea. So we'd go through magazines and see faces that we liked, that stood out to us, and we'd try and recreate them. I was utterly useless but we had a brilliant time! I was so inspired by what we could create and the fun we'd have along the way.

In all the jobs I've had in front of a camera, I've had so many different looks and products applied to my face, yet despite the huge number of hours I have spent having my make-up done or doing it myself, I've never got bored of it. Me and my glam squad could talk about beauty and make-up and hair and style and fashion all day long. We love it! But it's not the only reason we feel good about ourselves. It just brings us fun and excitement.

I still love experimenting with make-up. I love the creativity of playing with it and I've learned how to use it to enhance what I've got. But I've come to realise that it's not something I want to hide behind. I feel strongly that make-up shouldn't be a mask, or at least, not for me. Make-up can cause us to fall into the trap of trying to look a certain way, of hiding things, but that's not where the joy of it comes from. Sometimes when I do shows like *Dancing on Ice*, I'll glam up and I'll definitely wear more make-up than I would usually. Not because I'm trying to be someone entirely different; it's simply another side to me that I enjoy. That's another wonderful thing about make-up – I love the fact that you can look entirely different if you want to but not change the essence of who you are. That always remains. It's a bit like putting on a hat – it

It's about trying things out to figure out what makes us feel great.

doesn't affect the rest of my outfit or who I am. But it does add *something*.

I've written a lot about inner beauty and how we can reconnect with our authentic selves and get to a place where we feel happy in our own skin. Because I really believe that inner and outer beauty are inseparable – you have to feel good to look good. Now I want to celebrate the fun and creativity of make-up and style, and particularly how looking and feeling beautiful can work together. So let's get practical. I have a wealth of beauty tips from my years in the make-up chair, and I want to pass on some of those secrets.

There are a million brilliant beauty bloggers out there, creating amazing videos that demonstrate specific techniques in more detail than I can get into in a book. But while I think there are some principles of make-up that are really handy to know and fairly universal for everyone (and I'll tell you what those are), each of us is individual. We have different skin tones, textures, eye colours. As with everything, it's about trying things out to figure out what makes us feel great. Most of all, I hope I can inspire you to ditch all the outside pressure that can be put on us to look a certain way, and embrace a style of make-up that is right for you. Let's forget about this outdated idea that we have to look a certain way and think about beauty and make-up differently. We've spoken a lot about confidence and individuality. This section of the book is about expression and creativity.

MAKE-UP AS

MAKE-UP
AS RITUAL

arlier in the book, I wrote about rituals and how useful I find them in reminding me to take a moment for myself and still my busy brain. Your beauty regime is definitely something that you can treat as a ritual. In the morning, as you go about your routine, try to tune in to what's going on inside you. Look in the mirror at your reflection – and I mean at yourself as a whole and not just focusing on those eyebags or the hair you need to pluck out! Look yourself in the eye and take a few deep breaths, breathing deep into your stomach. Give yourself permission to just *feel* for a moment. Ask yourself, 'What do I want and what do I need today?'

As you start your skincare routine, breathe in and smell the cream you are applying. Maybe this is the time to set an intention for yourself for the day. You might like to use the action of putting on your mascara and eyeliner as a reminder to reflect on what you've seen, what you've learned that you're bringing with you into this moment. Applying your lipstick or lip balm might prompt you to think about what you'd like to say. If you put on earrings, maybe that could be a prompt to consider what you want people to hear. Is there anything that you need to be heard? Think about that inner truth inside.

This might sound like a big ask if mornings are busy in your house, but with practice you can do all this in a few seconds, and once you get the hang of it, you might find that it helps you to stay calm, even if you are rushing. If you prefer, use the time when you are taking your make-

Simply tell yourself that you're enough

up off at night, or rubbing in body lotion after a bath, to think about the things you are grateful for that day. As you wash away the dirt of the day, what else do you need to wash away and let go of?

Rubbing moisturiser into your skin and letting it sink in gives you an opportunity to say some nice things to yourself. As you're taking that moisturiser down over your torso, put your hands on your heart and say something that you need to hear, or simply tell yourself that you're enough. Looking after our skin in this way isn't just about trying to look a bit better: if you can reframe it as a ritual, then it can be an act of gratitude and kindness to your face and your body for taking you through the day.

BEAUTY TIPS
& TRICKS

beauty basics

One of the most positive, exciting changes in recent years for me has been how we have started to see a much more diverse representation of beauty. There's still a long way to go of course, but the fashion and beauty industries seem to be more aware of the fact that beauty comes in all shapes and sizes. The world is full of a dazzling array of beautiful humans, all with different skin colours and different bodies, and that is something we should celebrate as loudly as we can.

Historically, youth has always been a pillar of beauty, but that is something we are now challenging. There was once this idea that there was a short period in a woman's life where she was attractive and then it was over. But we're now evolving past that to realise that you can be beautiful at any age.

So what does that mean for the idea of 'classic beauty'? What, if anything, looks to stand the test

of time and can continue to inspire and guide us?

While our eyes are unique to each of us, framing them with dark eyelashes is enduringly popular. The effect the shape of our brows has on our face isn't going to change. We love to put a bit of colour on the lips and sometimes a hint of colour on the cheeks. This demonstrates that many of the fundamental ideas behind the concept of beauty are connected to good health. If you think about it, glowing skin, bright eyes and sometimes a flushed cheek are signs of being healthy and well.

It might sound obvious, but the most basic rule of beauty has to be to look after our health. We need to nourish ourselves and take care of our bodies to the best of our ability. This is where inner and outer beauty really come together. We know we need to drink plenty of water and eat good things so that our amazing, clever bodies have what they need,

and that we should get enough rest when we are able to.

We also need to be kind to our skin. To take off our make-up properly and moisturise. One of my most important beauty commandments is that I always wear factor 30 sun protection, whether it's winter or summer. That's definitely something I've come to understand the importance of as I've got older. Many moisturisers have sun protection built in, to avoid having to add another step to your morning routine, but most experts advise that you always wear specialised protection on top of that, and you should top up throughout the day, particularly in warm weather when you're more likely to sweat it off.

Finding a moisturiser that is right for you is important too. By the end of the day, does your skin feel tight and dry or is it shiny? Perhaps just around your nose and forehead? If your skin is on the oily side then you probably want a gel-based moisturiser, whereas if it's drier then something richer

and creamier might be better. There's a wealth of skincare information out there nowadays – entire YouTube channels, blogs and books are devoted to it. It can be overwhelming, but start simple and avoid introducing lots of new products at once.

My morning skincare regime is quite simple. I cleanse my face, put my moisturiser on and then clean my teeth, which allows just enough time for my moisturiser to sink in. Then I'll put my SPF on and allow time for that to be absorbed. I might use a serum or a primer and let that sink in while I get dressed. If you try to moisturise, then add sun factor and serum in quick succession, this will often be too much for your skin to absorb in one go. As I have got older, I feed my skin a little bit more, adding treat products like an overnight mask.

My skin isn't the same all the time. For example, my summer skin is very different to my winter skin. I try to pay attention to what my skin needs at different times of the year, whether that's more moisturising, more sun protection, less make-up, more coverage. And my skin also changes throughout the month. Before my period, my skin needs a lot more nourishing, and I always get spots around my chin and mouth. When I'm on my period, it feels like make-up doesn't sit very well on my skin. If this is something that might affect you, it's a good idea to keep a skin diary – it could give you a bit more insight into how your hormones are affecting you, what your skin might need at different times of the month, and could even stop you getting frustrated with your skin because you don't understand what it's up to.

how to know
& love your face

We see our faces so much more now than we did in the past because of all the time we spend talking into a computer screen and seeing ourselves on Zoom calls, taking selfies, trying to decide what to upload to social media, and being tagged in other people's feeds. So it makes sense that this has made us more conscious of the way that we appear to others.

Even the most confident among us will have bits of our faces or bodies that we focus on when we're having a bad day, that we wish we could change. I'm going to talk a bit about getting to know your face here, because I want you to love what you have, and have fun accentuating those things that make you, 'you'. But before I do, what I really want to say is that no one else looks at another person this way. It's important to remember that when anybody else looks at you, they see you as a whole. They might notice your smile and the way you look when you laugh, but they won't scrutinise the individual parts of your face in the way we would sometimes do to ourselves. So even while we're thinking about the shape of our eyebrows or the kind of eye make-up that suits us the best, we still need to remember to look at ourselves as a whole. As the unique individuals that we are.

One of the issues with social media is that the various filters give you a strange and unrealistic relationship with your face. You can smooth your skin and change the angle of your face, and that might be appealing for a moment, but it's not really you – it's not even what faces really look like. It promotes this one-size-fits-all idea of beauty as the norm, and in a way it undoes some of the great strides we've made towards recognising that outer beauty comes in so very many different forms.

We all deserve to have a positive relationship with what we see in the mirror, as we clean our teeth in the morning. This is the face that you were born with. This is the face that you have inherited from your ancestors, going back hundreds of years, that links you and them. This is the face that all those who love you look forward to seeing. There's no need to use make-up to turn yourself into someone you're not – ultimately, there's so much more joy in learning to love and celebrate the face that's uniquely yours.

In the following pages, I will mention various celebrities; women who may share your features and who you can therefore look to for inspiration. It might take a bit of practice to master a slightly different look – a flick or a cat's eye for example definitely needs a few goes and a steady hand! But just like showing the hairdresser a picture of someone whose hair is completely different to yours, trying to emulate the style of someone who is nothing like you is unlikely to bring out your best features.

eyes

What shape eyes do you have? It can be useful to figure out what suits you best, particularly if you want to experiment with new looks. Our eyes are the most unique part of our face; no two people have the same irises, even identical twins. If you can identify a celebrity with a similar eye shape to you, then you can borrow from the experience of their make-up artist and take inspiration from the colours and placement of the make-up.

Round eyes

If you've got round eyes, like Ashley Olsen, this means you can have a lot of fun with big flicks. Start your eyeliner right at the inner corner of your eye and go as far out as you like. Or use a darker shade in the crease of your eye and sweep it outwards, so it kind of pulls the shape of the eye out, if you like. Try focusing more on the top lashes when you put on your mascara and only applying the tiniest bit to the bottom ones. This sixties-inspired look can be very flattering for this eye shape.

Oval eyes

This is a versatile shape so you can really experiment. For example, try smoky shadow in the outer corners for a more intense look, or a simple slightly blended kohl liner to accentuate and celebrate the shape. This is a common eye shape so there is a lot of inspiration out there. Beyoncé, Mila Kunis and Keira Knightley all have oval-shaped eyes.

eyebrows

Eyebrows make such a difference to the structure of your face. There are so many different looks with eyebrows and I think it would be great to document all the fashion changes in eyebrow shape throughout history! In the 1990s, when I was a kid, Pamela Anderson's thin brow was all the rage, and I was so desperate to pluck my eyebrows but my mum told me, 'Absolutely do not do that, you'll regret it.' I'm so glad she did because now it's gone to the absolute polar opposite. When Cara Delevingne came on the scene, suddenly everybody was brushing their eyebrows up, wanting them to be thicker, and even using serums on them to make them grow.

Personally, I don't need my eyebrows to be perfect, but I think they look better when they're well groomed. My top tip is that if you're going to pluck them, just pluck from underneath, try not to pluck on top. Brush them up, pluck underneath, then slightly brush down along the top to smooth them down. Nilam Holmes is my eyebrow guru. She's an expert in making eyebrows look really beautiful but still natural, and she's got lots of tips available online.

When it comes to the colour of your eyebrows, just like the colour of your hair, it's your call. I think it's best to keep it quite tonal, maybe go one shade darker, or even one shade lighter. Fill in any gaps with an eyebrow pencil. You can get fixers that you apply with something that looks like a mascara wand just to hold it all in place and keep that groomed look. But apart from that, just let them be natural.

skin & bone structure

The first thing I want to say here is that everyone has pores. If we didn't have pores, our skin – the largest organ in our body – wouldn't be able to breathe. When you see a close-up photograph of someone's face and they have no visible texture at all, it's because the photo has been airbrushed or a filter has been applied.

We all get clogged pores, too. They can be reduced with a good skincare regime; exfoliating is key here to avoid the build-up of dead skin, with the extra bonus of eliminating dullness. But try to remember that no one else scrutinises our faces like we do. Who else's face have you ever examined in a magnifying mirror?! My skin is definitely not perfect – I still get breakouts from time to time – but that's just life.

There's been a real trend in recent years for contouring. There are so many kits and compacts on the market now, and lots of YouTube tutorials that show you how to use it to drastically change the appearance of the shape of your face. I contour along the hollows of my cheeks and just subtly under my jawbone to enhance or take away or shade a little bit. But I don't like to use contouring as a disguise or to the point where it becomes a mask.

The fashion for contouring means that some people think they should be adding lots of angles to their faces. That's their choice of course, but I think it can be a shame. Particularly if your face still has that slightly rounded softness of youth that's something to be celebrated. For example, if you have round apple cheeks then that is beautiful and you should enjoy it! Whatever age you are, focus on the best features of your face and learn how to enhance and celebrate them. There's no joy in trying to look like everyone else.

lips

There are so many differently shaped lips, all beautiful in their own way. As with every other feature, I think nature does it best, whether you have a defined cupid's bow, full lips, a thinner top lip – you have the lips that are meant for your face.

If you do want to use beauty products to enhance your lips, there are a couple of non-invasive cheats that might help: using lip primer before lipstick makes them look more polished; glossy lips always look bigger because the shine creates a curve, and I think paler lipstick also makes them look bigger. If you're confident with blending you can add a lighter shade to the middle of your bottom lip to plump it. The other trick is to dot a little highlighter on the cupid's bow which gives a bit more depth to that area. You can use lipliner outside of your lip rather than exactly on its edge to overline them, but you do need to be careful

as it can quite quickly look fake. Conversely, if you want to make your lips look smaller, then wear a lipstick that's closer to your skin tone or use matte lipstick.

I understand why people might want to make small changes, for example plumping lips or lifting the corners. But I do think that if you make big changes to your lips, whether with filler or overlining your lips dramatically, you need to make sure the balance is right. It's also worth bearing in mind that a plumped lip can cast a shadow on your teeth, making them look less white. But each to their own! I love how red lipstick is so iconic, and yet it can represent so many different things. It can be rock chick, it can be Hollywood starlet, it can be that chic French girl who just has a slick of lipstick on an otherwise bare face. It can be both classy and wild child.

Suffragettes wore red lipstick as a symbol of defiance, because at that

time you were still seen as a 'woman of the night' if you wore make-up. I love that. And then during the Second World War, wearing lipstick came to be seen as patriotic, with Elizabeth Arden creating shades with names like 'Victory Red'.

There are so many shades of red, so if you're looking to find the one that's best for you, head to the beauty counter to try some out. It will depend partly on your complexion – what make-up artists call your 'undertone', and whether that is cool, warm or neutral. The easiest way to determine your undertone is to look at the veins on your face, neck or wrists: if they're blue then you have cool undertones. In that case, blue-based reds (that look almost pink) are going to look amazing on you. If your veins appear green, then you're warm and more orangey reds suit you. And if you have both then you're neutral and you get the best of both worlds!

But it's also about what you feel works for you and your style. Remember that the same lipstick can look like many different lipsticks, depending on how you put it on. If you use your finger to dab just a bit on, pressing it into your lips, this will give you more of a casual look, like a lip stain. The same lipstick applied in layers with lipliner will give a more siren-ish look. Texture makes a difference too: a glossy red looks super-sexy whereas a matte lipstick is more sophisticated.

everyday make-up

My go-to products and how I use them has evolved and changed over time as I've got older and my tastes have changed, but the important thing is that they work for me, they make me feel good, and my make-up routine doesn't take all morning.

I'm not really a foundation kind of girl. Sometimes in the summer I'll just use an SPF cream (never forget that SPF!) that's got a bit of a tint, with some concealer where I need it – usually just around my nose or mouth. The thing to bear in mind here is that you've got to make sure that whatever moisturiser or serum you are using on your face before your concealer or foundation doesn't react with them. This will cause the make-up to 'roll' and it won't sit on your face properly. If you let your moisturiser sink in before adding anything on top, this is less likely to happen. I leave at least ten minutes before I start putting on my concealer.

Whatever skin coverage I use, I work it in until it looks even. I use concealer in the places where I need it and then a mineral powder afterwards because I find that doesn't build up. It goes on like a powder but then it kind of disappears, leaving a dewy rather than chalky finish. It's also something I can reapply as the day goes on, without it feeling like it's starting to cake or clog.

For my everyday look, I like to use a cream eyeshadow in a tone that's very neutral on my skin. It's slightly lighter than a bronzer in tone and it goes on really easily when I sweep it across my lid. I gently rub it in, and then my usual go-to is a bit of brown pencil liner, just on the edge of my lashes, so it doesn't create a heavy line. I always curl my eyelashes and I do like to use quite a lot of mascara, then often a little bit of bronzer all over and a tiny bit of rouge on the cheeks. My own preference is for a cream blush that I can rub in as it feels nicer on my skin and avoids adding layers of powder. I might use a tinted eyebrow fixer, some tinted lip balm and that's me ready to go.

So that's my routine. One of the reasons I like a more natural look is because I don't like to feel that my make-up is sliding around my face as the day wears on, that my skin can't breathe, or that I have to keep stopping to fix my make-up. If I'm going out in the evening, I might add a flick of liquid eyeliner, and tap a little bit of brown sparkle onto my eyelids. Sometimes I might be in the mood for a red lip, but that's it – it's quite simple, really.

We all have to figure out what works with our skin and makes us feel good. Sure, there are some great products out there and you can watch and read reviews to give you ideas, but there's not going to be a wonder product that works for everyone.

my make-up bag

Most of the time, when I'm at home, I don't wear make-up at all. When I leave the house to go to work, I don't put make-up on because I'll have it done at the studio. People are so used to seeing me on the telly with a full face of make-up under the bright lights, so outside of work someone will occasionally look at me and ask, 'Are you all right?' I don't mind; I know it's just because I look a bit different without make-up on.

If you usually wear a lot of make-up and you decide to change your look then you might find it takes people a while to adjust. That doesn't mean you look bad! I think it's important to get used to seeing yourself without make-up, so you don't feel like it's something you have to do.

The staples of my make-up bag, the things that have always remained the same, are really simple, and though I love to try out new things, it's these core products that I always have to hand and that I wouldn't be without. Everything else is an extra.

ESSENTIALS

- *DARK BLACK MASCARA*. I like a waterproof mascara as it doesn't budge, which is useful if, like me, you're quite an emotional person!

- Mascara goes on to curled eyelashes so much better, so I always keep an *EYELASH CURLER* to hand. It only takes a few seconds and it really opens up the eye.

- I use a *LIP SCRUB* to remove any roughness before I apply lipstick.

- No one likes that feeling of having dry, sore lips, so I always have a lovely *LIP BALM* in my bag.

- A good *CONCEALER* is so useful as you never know when you're going to have a breakout. Even on a good skin day, having something to cover a blemish or a bit of redness is good.

- I must have at least partly listened to my mum's advice about always putting *LIPSTICK* on, as a rosy, pinky lipstick is an essential for me. I can put a bit on my cheeks as well as on my lip and then I'm good to go!

getting creative

The brilliant thing about wearing make-up is that it can be a tool to help you draw out and celebrate different parts of your personality. Maybe you put on a red lip because it's Saturday night and you feel a bit sexy and vampy. Or perhaps it's a sunny day and so you trip out of the door in a summer dress, dusted lightly in bronzer. It seems funny that there is power to be harnessed from such a small thing, but it's almost like we are giving ourselves a signal, allowing ourselves permission to do something, to be something.

Quite often, before a night out, I think to myself, 'What do I need here? How do I want to feel?' Or if I'm going to a business meeting, I might think, 'Right! I need a bit of power here, so let's put a strong eyeliner on.' If I'm a bit tired, I'll use something to make my eyes look fresh and open, which will give me the kick up the bum that I need – by using make-up to make me look a little bit more alert, I'll start to feel it too.

Ever since I was a teenager, trying out make-up with my friends in my bedroom, I have loved the creativity that comes with it. Even if you are someone who knows exactly what suits them, who has their beauty and make-up regime down to a fine art, I would still urge you – even if it's just once in a blue moon – to try something a little different.

Of course, I'm not suggesting that you rush out and buy a trio of neon eyeshadows if your usual look is neutral tones. I just think that make-up is another tool that we have to play with, so every once in a while it's fun to, well, play! Try an eyeliner in a different colour, or teach yourself to do a 1960s-style flick, or ditch the big eyeliner altogether if that's your go-to and see how you feel about something more subtle. This can be a great way of reminding yourself that the main purpose of make-up isn't an undereye concealer that really hides those shadows, it's about having fun and making yourself feel good.

Sometimes, having an event or special occasion coming up that you are looking forward to getting dressed up for is good motivation to do this. When you have decided what you are wearing, go to a beauty counter and ask for some samples, or even find some looks you like in magazines or online and think about how they might translate to your face shape. Have some fun exploring different colours. Colour in make-up sometimes terrifies people, and you really don't have to go all out, but what about a pop of green or gold eyeshadow along the lash line or even underneath the eye, or lipstick in a colour you've never tried before? Tune in and ask yourself, 'What am I feeling and what do I want to project?' Probably

no one else will notice you've done your make-up differently, but the point is that *you* know, and it's a playfulness you've enjoyed. It's like wearing naughty knickers under your clothes – nobody knows but you, and it just makes you feel a bit different all day long!

Colours can represent many different things and therefore bring out certain feelings. Experimenting with colour doesn't have to be done on your face, of course. Maybe you want to bring certain colours into your life to remind you of particular things. I've put together a chart illustrating the meaning of colours. If you need to give yourself a little boost, a little reminder of something, then maybe choose a particular colour to wear to help you focus and remember an intention you set for yourself that morning. For example, wearing your yellow skirt might remind you to stay cheerful and positive when you are in danger of feeling overwhelmed, or looking down at your blue shoes in a meeting might help you to remember to be calm and confident.

Use the chart as a prompt.

RED	*Excitement* *Strength* *Love* *Energy*	ORANGE	*Confidence* *Success* *Bravery* *Sociability*
PINK	*Compassion* *Sincerity* *Sophistication* *Sweet*	PURPLE	*Royalty* *Luxury* *Spirituality* *Ambition*
YELLOW	*Creativity* *Happiness* *Warmth* *Cheer*	GREEN	*Nature* *Healing* *Freshness* *Quality*
BROWN	*Dependable* *Rugged* *Trustworthy* *Simple*	BLUE	*Trust* *Peace* *Loyalty* *Competence*
BLACK	*Formality* *Dramatic* *Sophistication* *Security*	WHITE	*Clean* *Simplicity* *Innocence* *Honest*

red carpet

Walking a red carpet is a big moment. It's so exposing, particularly when you are being photographed from all angles. When I do a photoshoot, I can leave the zip undone at the back if the clothes that have been chosen don't quite fit me, and they can smooth out wrinkles on a shirt in post-production. (Or wrinkles on your face, if that's what you want!) There are ways of cheating in photoshoots, but on a red carpet there's literally nowhere to hide. You have no control over the images that are being taken – usually with some pretty intense flash photography. Whenever I'm getting ready for a red carpet, whether it be hair, make-up or what I'm wearing, I have to think about something that works in 360 degrees. Something that I'm going to feel comfortable enough in; something that's not going to crease up when I'm sitting in the car on the way there. The funny thing about these events is that you might have got ready in a hotel room round the corner, but you still have to get in a car to pull up to the red carpet! If you then stand up and have great big creases across the lap of your dress where you've been sitting, it will really show up in the pictures.

When I'm deciding what to wear I have to consider the practicalities of the event, too. At an awards ceremony, like the National Television Awards, we'll be sitting down on chairs at the O2 sometimes for three hours, so you can't wear what I called a 'standing dress'. Some of my most glamorous *Dancing on Ice* dresses are standing dresses because you literally zip them up and that's it. There's no bending in the middle! It's not the most comfortable thing, but it's fun and looks great on TV, but definitely not what I would wear if I was going out and hoping to enjoy myself.

I have 'sitting heels' as well. Or 'taxi shoes', as some people call them! Shoes that I don't want to wear to a party because they're too high or uncomfortable but are absolutely fine if I'm hosting a show and only need to occasionally stand up for a minute or two to welcome a guest before I sit back down again. In terms of make-up, I have to think about what the emotion levels are going to be – I always find myself crying at the amazing, inspiring stories at the Pride of Britain Awards, and I don't really want to end up with mascara all over my face!

Before a red carpet event, I'll speak to my 'glam squad' girls – Ciler, Patsy and Danielle – to see what they think. Then I choose an outfit that's right for the occasion. Is it going to be a long gown? A shorter cocktail dress? For the BRITs you can wear something fun and short and a bit more rock and roll, but the BAFTAs, for example, is the kind of red carpet where a proper ballgown is needed. Once I know what I am wearing, we can start to plan my overall look for the night.

I used to worry more about what to wear to these big events, which

often meant I went for the more conservative option. However, I'm much more likely to have a bit of fun with my fashion now. These events only come round a few times a year and it's an enormous privilege to be invited and to get to wear these amazing dresses. So, my thinking now is: you might as well go all out!

Having said that, there are a few lessons I have learned (sometimes the hard way) about what doesn't work, particularly when you go to an evening event where there will be flash photography. It's annoying when you see unflattering photos and yet you know you actually felt great on the night. Once, on the red carpet of the BAFTAs, I was wearing a pink dress I felt really good in. Unbeknown to me, the flash of the cameras made my pretty pink Jenny Packham become translucent, and all anybody could talk about once the pictures came out was my massive pants under the dress.

how to prepare

I start thinking about how I'm going to wear my make-up for a big occasion once the dress has been chosen. Sometimes the gown speaks for itself and you think, 'OK, well, even though it's for the red carpet, let's just keep the make-up really simple.' Or the outfit is really simple and you think, 'Let's play! Let's push the boundaries a little more here.' Patsy, Ciler and I have a lot of fun pulling together images that we've seen, making mood boards and sharing them in our WhatsApp group.

Personally, I love a mood board, and I think it's really useful to see what other people have done. For example, the neckline on a dress can have a big impact on how you decide to wear your hair. So if your new dress has, say, a halter neckline and you're thinking, 'Hair up or hair down?', then you can trawl through Google images and find some pictures of people who have worn

that style and decide what you think works best. Quite often, hair can fight with a neckline. Sometimes you just want it to be really clean and off your face, but then if you're wearing a strapless dress and you have a longer style, it can be nice to wear your hair loose. There are no hard and fast rules here – so much depends on you as an individual. That's why it's great to look at different photos and what others have done and work out what you like.

At the moment, my personal taste for hair, even when I'm wearing a sophisticated frock, is a style that still has real movement to it. When everything else is done so perfectly, I like my hair to be a bit more natural, so it moves rather than being sprayed to stay fixed. This is actually the hardest thing to achieve, because while you don't want it to look overdone, you still don't want it to blow around if you're outside, and there's a lot of prep that goes into that. It comes down to finding the right products and getting texture into the hair so that you, and not the elements, have control of it on the night!

My prep often starts the day before a big event with my skin. I exfoliate my full body. I apply body moisturiser every single day anyway, especially now I'm getting older, but the night before an event, I'll go to bed like some sort of greasy chip covered in body oil and let it all sink in. The next day, I don't use body lotion except on my arms and on my neck and chest, the bits of skin that you can see, so as not to make my skin greasy in case I want to use tape.

Wherever I'm going and whatever the occasion, I always want to be able to see my skin underneath my base. It's more about the prep beforehand – the scrub, maybe a moisture mask, serum, a good primer – and dealing with any imperfection I have on the day with concealer. The layering is important and then perhaps warming up with a little bronzer over the top, with the result that you've then built up this base layer that sits really well and will last for a long time.

Years ago, I used to work in a beauty salon, so while I don't think I have particularly nice hands or feet, I do know that they look a lot better when they're cared for, whether you do that at home or in a salon. My personal preference is for natural nails. So, for me, Shellac is brilliant because it strengthens my nails without damaging them. I try really hard not to peel it off, but if I use it regularly, my nails tend to grow really strong. I keep the colour on my nails very neutral. It's rare nowadays that I'll wear anything other than a nude, because I feel like it's another element to my outfit that I just don't want to worry about.

I find it distracts from what I'm wearing. Really, I just want my toes and fingernails to look simple and healthy. That's at the core of all of my looks – clean, healthy and strong.

Before I start properly getting ready, I like to do a scrub to take off any dry skin on my lips and make sure they are really moisturised. I then usually go for a neutral lip line, followed by a stain and then blot to take it off, put more on and blot, and so on. I keep layering it so that the lipstick and my lips become friends. It gives it staying power, so even when the top layer rubs off in the first hour, you've still got the colour underneath.

For me, eyes are really important. Along with my trusty waterproof mascara, I wear fake eyelashes for those occasions where I want maximum impact. I used to wear strip lashes religiously. They're good for speed as you can just chuck them on and there are so many different types. Now, though, I tend to use individual eyelashes as I feel like I've got more control and I can place them where I really

need them. It's a lot more natural and just adds that little bit of drama. To finish off my eyes, whatever the look, I always use an eyebrow pencil, with a bit of fixer to keep them in place. I don't know about you, but I do find eyebrows like to have a wander around!

Ultimately, I think the aim when you are getting ready is to enjoy the process and then skip out of the door in anticipation of an enjoyable night – whether that's a friend's birthday or a big work occasion. You don't want to think about your make-up or what you are wearing again. It's like the Fairy Godmother has waved her magic wand and off you trot, and the only thing you've got to worry about is midnight, when you turn into a pumpkin (or when you realise you have to go home because the kids will be up at 6.30!). Cinderella wasn't thinking, 'Oh my gosh, my spot's going to come out. Do I need to do another layer of foundation in the bathroom at about 10.30?' Or, 'When I kiss Prince Charming, my lipstick's going to smudge all over his face!'

Big events don't come along that often, so let's embrace them and enjoy ourselves when they do. When you get dressed up, make sure it's fun. More than anything, make sure you're comfortable! If you love to dance, don't force yourself into those six-inch heels. There is no rule that says you have to wear heels if you don't want to.

Wear as much or as little make-up as you prefer. The memories you have of parties and events should be of the people who were there, the funny things that were said and the songs that got everyone on the dancefloor; not of trying to patch up your hanging eyelashes or your shredded feet while your friends are dancing on the bar.

TIPS FOR
SPECIAL EVENTS

- I never wear anything with shine in it because it tends to look terrible in a photo taken with a flash. So most of the fabrics I wear are matte. There might be the odd sequin, but my dresses will all have a *MATTE BASE*, which I think is much more flattering.

- Always check the *360-DEGREE VIEW* of your outfit, in the different positions you will naturally move into throughout the evening, and not just standing still in front of the mirror.

- When you see celebrities on the red carpet they are quite often *TAPED* into their dresses. If you are wearing something strapless, for example, you don't want any gaping that means you'll see a bit of underwear or bra or, God forbid, nipple. If I wear something that has the potential to move around a bit then everything gets taped to my skin so that it can't go anywhere. I just have to remember not to use body oil or moisturiser where the tape is going to touch my skin, otherwise it won't stick.

- *BODY MAKE-UP* can be really useful. You don't need to cover your whole body, but if you're wearing a backless dress and you've got a blemish on your back, it's good to have some to hand. For the big red carpet events, I use body make-up with a tiny bit of sheen in it, particularly on my collarbones to add definition and help them catch the light.

- As with shiny or shimmery clothes, it's a good idea to *BE CAREFUL WITH IRIDESCENT MAKE-UP* or glitter on your face if there's going to be lots of flash photography, as it can be reflected back at the camera, giving a weird halo effect. And some undereye concealers that have an illuminating effect are brilliant in everyday life, but can give you reverse panda eyes when the pigments reflect a strong flash.

- I am fond of *SUPPORT UNDERWEAR* to hold me in and help my dress fall in clean lines without clinging to any lumps and bumps caused by my underwear, but a note of caution... Underwear should never be so tight as to make you feel uncomfortable. This will probably stop you enjoying your evening and will be counter-productive as it will just squash everything in a way that won't look good under the dress anyway.

- Be careful if you're wearing *LIGHT UNDERWEAR* under something light because a flash can somehow, like X-ray vision, go through your dress and reveal your underwear for all to see, which is what happened to me at the BAFTAs.

- If you can, *GET YOUR CLOTHES ALTERED PROFESSIONALLY* so that they fit perfectly. It tots up so is best saved for special occasions but if you're in between sizes like me, it makes the world of difference to how confident you feel in your clothes.

- Bring a *HANDBAG* with a few essential items: a thin compact with fine milled powder and a small brush, your lipstick, a tissue and mascara.

ageing

Back in 2006, I was covering the *Happy Feet* premiere in Leicester Square and was interviewing the stars. I had to wrap up quickly and get across town to the Children's BAFTAs because I was nominated. But the car that was supposed to take me there didn't turn up and they weren't allowing anyone into Leicester Square. A photographer who had been taking pictures on the red carpet said, 'Holly, aren't you meant to be at the BAFTAs?' I explained that I was a bit stuck and he offered me a lift. I did my make-up in the car, then jumped out and off I trundled down the red carpet, wearing a dress I'd bought on holiday in Dubai and a necklace with a heart on it that Fearne Cotton had given me. That's youth, isn't it!

One of life's ironies is that we can either have the radiance and energy of youth or the wisdom and self-knowledge of age. We live in a culture that prizes youth, but most of us need time to really get to know and like ourselves. When it comes to ageing, we just need to repackage how we view it. There are so many more women out there now in the public eye who are still owning their beauty, who are sexy and stylish well after the point when women used to become essentially invisible to society.

Ageing is a real privilege. There are many people who never got there; who, no matter how stunning they were in their youth, didn't have the opportunity to see their face change as they became older. Your face is your story of where you've been and how you've lived, and it's unique to you. It takes a very strong woman indeed to not care a jot about ageing, to not sometimes wish her skin still looked how it did at twenty, so I'm not asking you to wholeheartedly love your lines and your wrinkles. I just think that we can try to accept that while our faces and bodies change as we age, it doesn't mean that we aren't still beautiful.

I'm in my forties now and I can see the changes in my face. I know that my skin needs a lot more love, particularly hydration. If I have a late night or if I've been out drinking, I definitely notice it. My face will just eat my make-up – it doesn't sit as well on my skin. So I have started to look after my skin a bit more, to not take it for granted, and I've found that different products now work better for me than those I used when I was younger.

I never used to have facials, but now I have a collagen wave once a month, which is a sort of electrical treatment that uses radio waves to encourage the cells to produce collagen. I notice the difference and it does make me feel better and more confident – I'd be lying if I said it didn't. That doesn't mean it's the only place my confidence comes from, though.

Will I have any beauty procedures, or cosmetic procedures as I get older? The answer is, I don't know yet. I probably will indulge in a few – I'm reserving the right to decide how I feel about all that when I get there. What I do know for sure is that I want any decision to come from a positive place where I enjoy getting a little boost, and not a negative place where I think I need to be 'fixed' outwardly in some way.

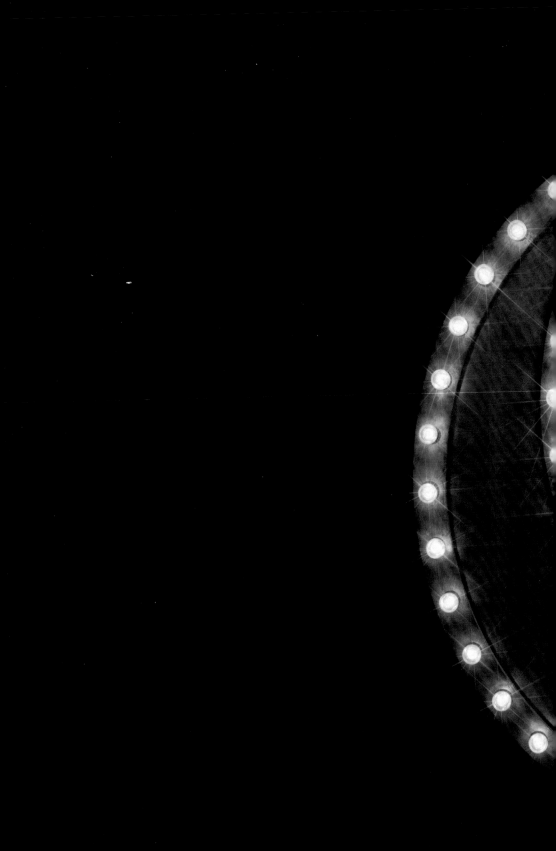

hormones

There's something overwhelming about being a teenager and suddenly finding yourself with a face that's changing and skin that's unpredictable, at the same time that unfamiliar hormones are raging around your system and all you want to do is work out who it is you fancy.

When I was a teenager, I remember using Clean & Clear or Clearasil and thinking that unless it was burning my skin, it wasn't doing anything. I was obsessed with that nail-varnish-remover feeling. But actually the most important thing when you are that age is hygiene and not messing with pH balance, because what's happening as you go from being a child to an adult is that your body starts producing more sebum. Using astringent products to strip the skin upsets the pH balance and really doesn't help at all.

It's also a good idea to create good habits in terms of looking after your skin at a young age. You don't need a rigorous, extreme routine involving loads of products. It comes back to hygiene again. You may just need a suitable cleanser, good flannels or muslin cloths and a moisturiser. There are so many brands that create specialised products for younger skin, and that's a great place to start.

Pregnancy can really change your skin. Or at least, it did for me. When you're pregnant, your temperature rises. You get hotter and more flushed. I was very hormonal when I was pregnant with all three of my kids and I don't think my skin's ever gone back to how it was before. I mentioned earlier how I notice a difference in my skin at different times of my cycle, and I feel like I have become more sensitive to my hormones ever since giving birth.

If you are pregnant and experiencing anything like this

and still want some coverage on your skin, consider using a tinted moisturiser. Though really, if you are feeling hot and flushed, then the less you put on your skin, the better. You should already include SPF as part of your skincare regime, but so many first-time mums forget and then they develop pigmentation. Pregnancy hormones can already cause melasma, another kind of skin pigmentation, which means SPF is even more important during pregnancy if you want to avoid darkening patches of skin.

It wasn't until I discovered hormone expert Alisa Vitti that I discovered how much skin changes during your menstrual cycle. For example, skin plays up by producing more oil during your period, so calming, hydrating products are best. And around days 25–28 of a cycle, the skin is oilier.

Through her work, I also learned just how much the skin changes during perimenopause and menopause. During the former, it can break out into acne, which can be combatted through good skincare and diet. And during the latter, the skin loses its elasticity and hydration is very important to counter that.

Bodies are extraordinarily complex. Sometimes I feel overwhelmed by just how much there is to learn about hormones and the body, but the more you learn, the more you can tune in to yourself and be at your best, whatever your hormones are doing!

most of all, love yourself

Now that I've shown you every nook and cranny of my make-up bag and shared a few tips and tricks, I hope you've found one or two things helpful. Perhaps my biggest take-home message is that make-up has to work for you, with you, as a tool to highlight and enhance. Make-up and what we do with it comes down to that wonderful thing: choice. So make the most of it and always have fun with what you do. Make-up is not meant for you to hide behind.

Feel free to create a whole new face with clever make-up placement, but always let your true self shine through and ensure that you're in control… Your face, your rules, your identity. Your face is loved by all those whom you love. Perhaps it's the face that, from the second they laid eyes on you, your parents felt such an overwhelming surge of love, that they wondered how they had any left for anyone else. Or maybe it's the face your children turn to for guidance and protection. It's the face your friends look to for support and comfort, it's the face your partner wants to hold and stare into the eyes of… There's a lot of love out there for your face, maybe you could add to it with a bit of love from yourself.

*'You've always
had the power…'*

Glinda to Dorothy in *The Wizard of Oz*

epilogue

I thought I'd finish by leaving you with some wishes for your onward journey. I want you to feel safe and protected, if not by those around you, then by the boundaries you set for yourself. I want you to be heard and, most importantly, understood. I feel that if you have clarity of self, then those around you will find it easier to understand you. I hope you feel the power that was there all along – you always had everything, you just needed some encouragement.

I hope that all genders are recognised at the same level as their male counterparts. I hope that women continue to strengthen the bonds of sisterhood with one another, to help and support and push one another forward. I hear your call and I'm here to help. Collectively, we will continue to grow and evolve.

Remember that everything is a phase that will pass, but in passing it will leave us more experienced and wiser. Then, the moment we feel we have it all figured out, this too will pass... making room for more growth! Change isn't linear and you will have good days and bad. I find ultimately both are beneficial; keep moving forward.

I hope that you can look at your reflection and find acceptance, gratitude and beauty. Be kind, patient and respectful to others and to yourself. Find your community but don't get lost in it. Listen to children; they just know. Listen to yourself, too; you just know.

This world moves so fast and asks so much of us, so stop and look up... Find your moon... Breathe... It's beautiful out there...

Love,

Holly x

'This is one of my favourite photos of myself and Dan taken right at the beginning of our relationship. I love it because it feels like we're walking into the rest of our lives…'

ACKNOWLEDGEMENTS

I began this journey with a clear idea of exactly what I wanted this book to be, what I wanted to say and even how I wanted it to look, but I had absolutely no idea how I was going to turn all my thoughts into words on a page! It's fair to say that my confidence as a writer was very low and I don't think I believed that I had the capability at all.

In the past I've always written with my brilliant sister, to whom the art of writing comes so naturally. Consequently, I assumed that in order to get this book to print, I'd have to work closely with a ghost writer for guidance and help getting the words down. I think being dyslexic also played its part in my self-doubt as a writer. I'm not going to say that dyslexia is a problem for me now, because it's not, and I'd actually go as far as saying I actually love being dyslexic. I feel part of a very special group of people who find their own unique blueprint to learning, reading, writing and studying. However, there are some preconceived limitations that are unavoidable, and I guess attempting to write a book alone felt like it just might be a bridge too far. So in order to take the idea to publishers, I started to record voice notes... long ramblings of thoughts which poured out from my head.

When I was ready, I sent them on to Felicity Blunt at Curtis Brown. I have never been more nervous or scared about anything, not to mention completely mortified at the thought that Felicity might find my recordings, at best, lacking in depth, and at worst, someone playing at being a writer but failing horribly. Much to my shock, she said she liked what she had heard! She introduced me to some publishers, at which point I met my editor Zennor Compton. I owe so much to these two wonderful women, who from the get-go encouraged me to write by myself. There is real power in someone believing in you. It gives you wings to fly, or in this case to write.

Zennor: how many calls, emails, texts, zooms? Thank you for everything. You have helped me in so many ways. You gave me the confidence to do this and I've loved the process. There's no going back now...Thank you really doesn't cut it!

Felicity: thank you for getting the ball rolling and for your encouragement and unwavering belief in me. Had it not been for you, this would all still be sitting in a voice notes folder. Martinis all round I think...And I know just the person to make them!

Thank you too to everyone at Penguin Random House, especially Olivia Allen, Meredith Benson, Venetia Butterfield, Charlotte Bush, Claire Bush, Callum Crute, Etty Eastwood, Emma Grey Gelder, Linda Hodgson, Roisin O'Shea, Claire Simmonds and Joanna Taylor. Thank you, early readers Ateh Jewel and Josephine Chick.

There are so many people to thank, so many who have played their part, not only to get this book onto the shelves, but also who have inspired what is on its pages.

Dan: my hand was made to hold yours. Thank you for your love and never-ending support. Thank you for filling our home with laughter...OK, you taught me jokes! Love you to the moon and back.

Harry, Belle and Chester: you are true beauty. You came to teach me and I still have so much to learn. I love you so much. Stick together and always be kind. Belle, you read the first chapter of this book and said it made you feel safe. In that moment, you gave me the courage to believe in myself as a writer. Thank you.

My parents: when you have good soil beautiful things grow, right? Thank you Mum and Dad for giving me the best start and great foundations on which to build – love you.

My sister: for being you, for helping me, for guiding me, for inspiring me. I'd be lost without you Kel…My earth angel.

To my mother in law Sandra, Uncle Nuts Nuts, Auntie Wee Wee's, Auntie Francesca and Jem, for giving me Dan and everything that followed…

Vicky Staines: Auntie Vick – can you imagine the state I'd be in if it wasn't for you? Both Dan and I would be all over the place! You dot the 'i's and cross the 't's before I've even thought to write it down. Love you!

My Roxy management girls and my PA Nicola Boddington: talk about hitting the ground running! Thank you for swooping in and being, quite simply, bloody fantastic. My publicist Laura Sinclair, who always has a calm head and clarity of judgment, even when all around her have lost theirs.

My Wylde Women: you know who you are…Especially Claire Skinner for her instinct on everything. For being head of comedy when it's needed and for conjuring up Whiskey Sours on demand. Louise, my hair forever! Sass, India, Jo: the adventure has only just begun…I can hear the call of the Wylde.

Jon Gorrigan and your brilliant team: thank you for always taking insane pics…You are so very clever!

All the women in my life, my girlfriends, especially Nic Appleton, Shiarra Bell, Christine Lampard, Niki De Metz, Emma Bunton, Sarah Shenston, Hannah Peckham, Fearne Cotton, Davina McCall, Emma Nye, Sophie Renwick, Juliet Denison. Beauty shines from you all. You are all goddesses. I'll run with you throughout my life, by your side. I'm here for you. You are the helium in my balloon – holding me up, buoyant – and when I breathe you in, the laughter follows. I love the bones of you all.

My glam girls: the glitter kittens! Patsy O'Neill for painting my face and patching me up physically and mentally. Ciler Peksah for being the rock star of the blow-dry, whose words are as soothing as any treatment she puts in my hair. Danielle Whiteman: watching you blossom has been a joy…Keep believing in yourself. You've got this so go be your brilliant self. An Tran: beautiful mamma and the best nail technician in the business.

The triangle of wisdom who have given me so much: Emma Lucy Knowles, Will Williams, and Selda Goodwin. You three have filled my toolkit for life…Thank you.

There are so many women I want to thank who continue to inspire me: Vanessa Hill, Emma Gormley, Kalpna Patel-Knight, Emily Page, Lucy Newman, Ellie Cole, Kerry Burch, Juliette Bacon, Ali Donnelly, Eva Speakman, Jill Neilson, Katie Roake, Mrs Williamson, Claire Mellon, and Midwife Fredette. And to Charlotte Hannaford…I'd be lost without you.

And to all the amazing men who have helped me and

been true allies along the way. Phil Schofield: thank you for your friendship, the belly-aching laughs and your unfaltering belief in me. To Stephen Mulhern, Jake Humphrey, Bradley Walsh, Ant & Dec, Leigh Francis, Martin Frizell, Chris Bellinger, Christopher Pilkington, Kevin Lygo, Peter Weiss, Antony Perlmutter and Nik Speakman...thank you.

Perhaps the biggest thank you of all goes to you for picking up this book in the first place. Time is precious and the fact that you have chosen to spend some of yours among these pages means the earth. During the writing process, someone asked me what success with this book would look like, such as having a number one bestseller, for example. I had one answer. My hopes and dreams for this book was always for it to be something that gets passed on from friend to friend through recommendation. I really hope that some of it resonates with you, and that maybe some of it will stay with you.

Thank you all x

resources

WYLDE MOON

For further reading and to take a deep dive with me go to www.wyldemoon.co.uk

MENTAL HEALTH SUPPORT

BACP
(British Association for Counselling and Psychotherapy)
www.bacp.co.uk

CALM
(Campaign Against Living Miserably)
Helpline: 0800 58 58 58
www.thecalmzone.net

MIND
Infoline: 0300 123 3393
www.mind.org.uk

NHS
www.nhs.uk/service-search/mental-health

CRYSTALS

Emma Lucy Knowles
www.emmalucyknowles.com

EYEBROWS

Nilam Holmes
www.eyebrowqueenpro.com

HORMONES

Flo Living – Alissa Vitti
www.floliving.com

MEDITATION

Beeja Meditation with Will Williams
www.beejameditation.com

SOUND HEALING

Selda Soul Space
www.seldasoulspace.com

picture credits